CHRIS HOWKINS

TREES
AND
PEOPLE

IN SURREY AND BEYOND

PUBLISHED BY
CHRIS HOWKINS

First published 1999

© Chris Howkins 1999

PUBLISHED BY
Chris Howkins,
70 Grange Road,
New Haw,
Addlestone,
Surrey,
KT15 3RH

PRINTED in England by
Unwin Brothers Ltd.,
The Gresham Press,
Old Woking,
Surrey.
GU22 9LH

ISBN 1 901087 10 7

Plane trees (Platanus x hispanica) over the Wey Navigation at West Hall, Byfleet. These are unusual for having been coppiced. Before becoming a National Trust property all the waterside vegetation and trees were cut back regularly.

Planes, despite being the commonest street tree in the world, do not feature much in Surrey although a new avenue in Sopwith Drive, Brooklands, Byfleet, should be grand in years to come.

CONTENTS

Great Fosters, Egham.
C. Howkins 1982 ©

INTRODUCTION

It was a grand walk down through the Devil's Punch Bowl amid golden Birch and Bracken, on a Saturday afternoon, free from school. We got to Thursley church and I was taken in to see. I'd never thought of a church as being historic or interesting, didn't even have much notion of history. It was just sometime pre-granny. I was, therefore, in no way prepared for the sight of those great tree trunks straddling the nave as they lifted the belfry high above their heads. Medieval! What, from the Middle Ages? Could anything be left from then? Into the chancel and there I was shown the little Saxon windows, complete with their wooden frames, shown where the Normans came along and painted little red flowers on the plaster like a wallpaper design. As I peered through those windows so I looked into our social history with interest for the first time. They really captured my imagination and ever since I have explored the world of trees and woodwork and the ways people used to live.

This book is designed to share some of the discoveries of the various ways in which people have interacted with trees. It's a social history, about people like ourselves who through work or pleasure or spiritual beliefs find themselves involved in the world of trees. Many readers will have gone off to infant school clutching a handful of Lambs' Tails, Sticky Buds or Pussy Willow to get their gold star on the chart. Others will remember playing conkers or scrumping apples. Even the most urban reader will be familiar with Christmas Trees and Holly at the end of the year and that's before considering the trees that made our musical instruments, sports equipment and the woodwork in our homes. Trees play an important part in all our lives.

LEFT: The English Country House, in this case, Great Fosters at Egham, with its rich red Tudor brickwork, fits confortably into the landscape, amid its sheltering foil of Beech trees. Being forest trees they are large enough to prevent the architecture becoming overpowering. Similarly, the clipped Yews are on a scale large enough to complement the great house without intimidating its visitors. With their important degree of formality, they add considerably to the emotional atmosphere of the approach and throughout the year provide strong colour to match the brickwork. The *Magnolia grandiflora* up the wall gives that final touch of the exotic. This is the artistry at which the the English have made themselves real masters.

The interaction between trees and people, through the ages, is a vast and fascinating study to which this is only an introduction. In order to keep it manageable inspiration has been drawn from the social history of only a small area of the country: the county of Surrey. For this purpose that is defined as the area administered currently by Surrey County Council. That part of Middlesex which is now the Borough of Spelthorne is therefore included but the south London Boroughs are not. The material has been retrieved from files amassed over the last thirty years and this has dictated the the choice of trees and their stories. Thought has also been given to readers from beyond that boundary by choosing material that will have counterparts in their own districts. I was told once by Alan Mitchell that there are over 1,500 different trees in Surrey so this is just a tiny selection.

Trees fulfil a multitude of roles and these change from century to century. Today there is an emphasis upon various aspects of public 'amenity value' and upon wildlife conservation. Neither is entirely new. Trees have always been valued for their aesthetic qualities, whether in Celtic nature poetry, a Roman garden or the front lawn of a country house. The forerunner of nature conservation was the provision of game-cover for the chase and the shoot. In general man's relationship with trees falls into three broad divisions: aesthetic values, economic values and spiritual values. These will now be developed a little further.

AMENITY VALUES

It's early September in the year 1840 and the first leaves are turning yellow in the great Willow beds all along the Thames. You join the other sightseers gathered by the roadside, on the higher ground just above Walton Bridge. Opposite is Mount Felix, the grand home of the 5th Earl of Tankerville. He's just had the house rebuilt by Charles Barry, who you'd think would be busy enough rebuilding the Houses of Parliament. It is indeed a grand house, built in an Italianate style, and includes such distinctions as the first

E. Hawkinow
1983
Watts Chapel, Compton.

Roman tiles made in Britain. The Duke of Devonshire has been to pay it a visit but it wasn't so much the architecture that caught his eye so much as a tree. Lady Tankerville has a 50ft palm tree in her palm house and the Duke of Devonshire is employing Joseph Paxton of glasshouse fame. Now wouldn't that palm look just wonderful in a new glasshouse at Chatsworth? Her Ladyship has been persuaded to part with her palm.

Paxton has been down to organise its removal to Chatsworth and that has been much talked of locally. Wagon builders, wheelwrights, carters, they've all been contacted because this load, over 50 feet long, weighing 12 tons and being 8ft 4in round, is going to need its own specially built wagon, pulled by a team of no less than eleven horses. Now's the day for it to begin its long journey of 180 miles to Chatsworth in Derbyshire. The load is so immense that toll gates on the turnpikes are having to be removed to make way for it. Such expenses will total £1,000 for the journey but what does that matter when you're the Earl of Devonshire and you're getting what you want?

That's the most extreme example that I know, from Surrey, of the lengths to which someone has been for their desire of a tree. After all, it was only for its 'looks', it's there to please and to impress - those of the appropriate class whose carriages might just wend their way to Chatsworth, during

'the season'. It's a far cry from the days when most landowners viewed their trees solely from an economic standpoint. Nevertheless, the Duke of Devonshire was continuing a fashion which was by his time already mature. It was the English who pioneered the use of trees collectively in the landscape, not only to enhance it but to help create totally new scenes of hills and vales and lakes. Capability Brown is best known for that but designers like William Kent and Charles Bridgeman were there before him. Both of them worked at Claremont in Surrey, where Brown was the architect of the house. (The 'Landscape Garden' is open to the public courtesy of the National Trust). Brown's other landscape work included Clandon, Peperharow, and Gatton Parks. His famous tree 'clumps' at Gatton are to be replanted; the last survivors having been destroyed by the Great Storm of October 1987. Restoration is now well advanced in the county's finest landscaped park, Painshill, which is also open to the public.

Painshill, Claremont and their once famous neighbours at Esher, Woburn, Portmore and Oatlands, all made fine use of our large scale native trees, such as Beech, Oak, and Elm. There were fewer foreign trees or 'exotics' to choose from in those days. Nevertheless they made good use of the best - so much so that Weeping Willows and Cedars of Lebanon have been taken very much to heart by the English. Today it's a different story. So much of the amenity planting comes under the auspices of planning authorities etc. that there is immense pressure to plant only British natives. It's supposed to be good for the wildlife. Gardeners and foresters can list hundreds of species of wildlife that can decimate foreign trees! There are, however, valued wildlife species which do depend upon the natives, usually when the trees are mature. In a county like Surrey, where there are more trees than in any other county, there is room to use both. People count too.

What is important is getting the right trees in the right place for the right reason. The open countryside is not the place for exotics; the large Copper Beech out in the fields at Compton is a nasty dark blot in the green and spreading vale. In a red brick townscape it's a different matter. Copper Beeches can add depth of tone, highlight the sunshine on the bricks and, most importantly, being so large they make the buildings look smaller, keep a human scale to the scene. The skimpy little Birch trees so often employed in current townscaping will never do that. They are not the right trees in the right place at all. Big forest trees are much needed in built-up areas, root-room permitting, to keep this sense of scale. That's what is so good about Woking - so often denegrated as a concrete jungle, which it is when you fly over the top, but from the air the suburbs hardly show; Maybury, Horsell, St. Johns, etc. all nestle away under a green canopy. Here you can see the changing seasons, enjoy bud-break and blossom and autumn colours and have a garden full of bird song. It is fortunate that the Council appreciates this and works to perpetuate it.

Similarly, Woking Borough Council takes a responsible view of its land having once been of world importance in the history of horticulture and would like to perpetuate it. Its row of Black Birches, *Betula nigra*, left from the nursery days, is being killed by honey fungus and it is trying to grow some more. Sadly these trees don't seem to like Woking and are proving difficult! This makes the mature ones all the more precious. Foreign they may be but they are part of Woking's social history and are appreciated for being that.

Not all Councils see it that way. There was room for twelve trees at a Community Centre that was being modernised whereupon the Council stipulated they should all be native species - not quite what the community had in mind. Eventually the Council relented - eleven natives and one exotic. A Golden Robinia was chosen; something that can make a cheerful splash of sunshine in suburban areas

ROADS

On the main road at Milford there are some mature Flowering Cherry trees, colourful at blossom time and again in the autumn. These and many others were planted in 1934 when the County Council had three new major road schemes coming to completion: the Guildford and Godalming By-pass; the Leatherhead By-pass and the Dorking By-pass. The Council minutes record that these were the last of ten such schemes for which they had been responsible in the last ten years. They amounted to some forty miles and trees had been, or were about to be, planted along them. Even in those days it was difficult to please everyone. Discord arose where the Guildford road crossed Lord Antrim's land and The Roads Beautifying Association had submitted a planting proposal that included shrubs such as Azaleas. The sub-committee wanted it all pegged out for them to visit, view and decide. They decided against on the grounds that it provided *"far too many ornamental shrubs such as azaleas which have a short-lived flowering stage."* They did not, however, reject on the same grounds the hundred and fifty small Rhododendrons *"generously supplied"* by Mr. Lionel de Rothschild for the Dorking By-pass, nor his replacements for those he'd given for the Guildford/ Godalming By-pass but which had died. The Council did buy trees. They came from Slocock's famous Woking Nursery at the following rates:- for Leatherhead £14-4s-9d, for Dorking £65-4s and for Guildford £264-14s-3d. The total expenditure was far less than what was spent on the pair of scissors with which the Minister of Transport, Mr. Leslie Hore-Belisha M.P., was to cut the opening ribbon! The Council also decided it was time to start employing an officer *"to inspect and generally supervise the maintenance of the trees and shrubs."* They allocated £60 to provide him with a motor-cycle and sidecar plus a weekly wage of £4.

Today we would still have heated debate about colourful shrubs and trees along our roads. There seems to be a good balance, on the whole in Surrey. Massed ground-cover roses produce colour and scent up the central reservation of the A320 south of Thorpe Park. Out in the countryside the plantings are predominantly of natives. There are still daft moments though. Pine trees suppress ground vegetation totally, so why plant them on embankments where erosion is least desirable? There are some on St. Peter's Way at Chertsey where there was massive subsidence problems during construction.

7

RITUAL VALUES

The ritual values of the trees began thousands of years ago when peoples endowed the trees with spiritual forces. These forces are difficult to explain today, partly because we do not know enough about the early beliefs and partly because such allegiances are far removed from the present lives and thinkings of today's people. Nevertheless, there is a growing number of people who are once again returning to 'nature' for their spiritual and emotional support. It would seem that in the past the tree spirits were not always supportive, and needed supplication rituals to ensure their goodwill. They were powerful forces and heeded with respect. Today they are best summed up with words such as gods and goddesses, although these must be used in their widest sense. Very importantly, people believed they were descended from tree ancestors, and had appropriate creation myths to substantiate this belief (see Ash and Elm entries). Another significant belief in those pre-Christian times was the notion that after death the soul went on to another world - but could come back. Therefore degrees of 'ancestor worship' become apparent in studying the early folklore of our trees.

Folklore is a word chosen for being respectable and serious. To many it is 'superstition' which by the dictionary definition would be right, except, in popular usage the word is used to convey a degree of silly triviality. That's inappropriate. The beliefs were once highly significant to our ancestors. At great expense they made votive offerings of gold torcs etc. into the sacred pools, to stun the delving archaeologists of today. Similarly, they expended time and skill creating wooden effigies of the gods, which we know of from preserved remains in acid peat bogs etc.

The tree that is still the focus of the most prevalent of the ancient practices is the Elder. Country people still treat it with respect, still ask with rhyme and gesture before they cut it, still ban it from bonfires, and so on. There are firms of garden contractors who will not cut Elder even for money, firms of undertakers who will put Elder twigs in the coffin on request, and even the big firms of commercial bakers still produce 'split crust loaves', not to mention the Christianising of an older practice for 'hot cross buns'. (The story of the Elder is available as a separate booklet.)

With the coming of Christianity there was a need to destroy the ancient allegiances or to convert them to Christian use. Ancestor worship was suppressed although ancestors are still very important today to the Mormons and their Church of Jesus Christ and the Latter-day Saints. There are a lot of others who say 'touch wood' when they say something risky - calling up their ancestors from the other world to support them. This aspect of tree worship was too powerful to suppress and so it became Christianised as a symbolic touching of the wood of Christ's Cross - calling upon the support of Jesus. Fertility rites, leading to good harvests and successful stock rearing, to ensure future prosperity, were suppressed too. People were encouraged to trust in a new caring and benevolent god who would decide for Himself whether you would prosper or not. Therefore it became important to say thank you, giving rise to harvest celebrations. Pre-Christians did not have these in the same way; instead, they performed supplication or fertility rituals ahead of harvest time to ensure success. Harvests were, therefore, accepted almost as an inevitability because the gods had been pleased.

These beliefs gave a sense of security in a dangerous world where death, disease and disaster were ever present. Giving them up in the name of a new God challenged that security. People followed both faiths for hundreds of years. The Christians founded Chertsey Abbey in the 7th century yet as late as the 11th century tree worship was still so prevalent that King Cnut (r.1016-1035) resorted to banning the sacred groves by the law of the land. In the 12th century, when the west door was installed at St. Peter's church, Old Woking, the smith added symbolic ironwork illustrating the pagan Norse style beliefs being suppressed by the Cross. Obviously he expected the parishioners to be so familiar with the old beliefs that they would read his message on the door: leave the old beliefs outside as you step into the church and the new belief in Christian salvation. The door is still there for you to see.

PRACTICAL USES

All native trees, without exception, had their practical uses. Their timbers have varying characteristics and these were exploited to the full in the past. There's more to a tree than its wood though. Pliant shoots, such as those of the Willows, were cut for baskets and cradles while those of the Walnut made hair dye. Thicker rods, especially of Hazel, were woven into hurdles and wattle panels. Leaves of the Ash were dried and used to adulterate tea while those of the Elm were cut in late summer to use for winter fodder. Elder flowers made wine, cordial and face washes. Nuts and fruits not only provided food but medicines and dyes, such as a lustrous black for greying hair from Elderberries. Some bark yielded dye, food and medicines too. Most of the main British trees had about four dozen different uses, some a lot more, while the smaller, less common trees had fewer but nevertheless were not neglected. When a tree was felled or blew down it was possible to use up every bit of it. With so many hundreds of uses to choose from only a tiny selection have been highlighted in this book. All in all I hope this book dispels a five-year-old's definition that "*A tree is a lump of wood wiv leaves on.*"

DATING TREES

The age of a tree holds a strange fascination over people. The formula used by Alan Mitchell for estimating this, and it is only an estimate, is to measure the girth of a mature tree 1.5m above ground level and allow 2.5cm for every year of growth. Young trees will grow faster. Very old trees slow down. Some he describes as "hares and tortoises" because they do not conform to the formula anyway. Estimates can be very wrong as was proved so many times after the Great Storm of 1987 which enabled growth rings to be counted when a victim was being sawn up afterwards. A large healthy Oak, 6m round, is likely to be about 250 years old. Similar reservations can be expressed about the formula for dating hedges. These are estimates to give a guide which can be valuable to conservationists but there is still a need for diligent research through the documentary records before anything like an informed opinion can be expressed.

WHAT ABOUT YEW TREES ?

Ancient Yews become hollow so it is never possible to bore out a core and count the rings. Consequently, the ages of these trees have been wild guesses. Using documentary evidence for examples measured at intervals over a long period, Allen Meredith has calculated, from the growth rates, a formula by which to estimate the age. This has been ridiculed and at the same time it has convinced many serious scientists, despite their initial doubts. The findings please those with a romantic imagination, for some of the trees would appear to be thousands of years old, just like California's Bristle Cone Pines. There does not seem to be any reason to discount totally the findings but many people would prefer more work to be completed on the matter. The following chapter on Yew trees takes the 'ancient' viewpoint. There are three, more conservative, formulas which can be used. In the case of the Tandridge Yew they give ages of 845, 880 and 1,030 years, as measured in 1996. Meredith's formula arrived at 2,500 years.

OPEN TO DOUBT ?

One of the Yews that is suddenly getting cited as 'ancient' grows at Waverley Abbey; just the right sort of place. It does indeed have a very fine spreading head of branches but the *bole* is not on the same scale as the other supposedly ancient Yews in Surrey. More importantly, would the monks have built the east wall of their church right up against the trunk? If so, where are the scars from the removal of the western branches? Even more importantly, how is it that the roots grow up over the foundations of the church wall. The Abbey was Dissolved in 1536 and used as a quarry for building Loseley; surely the Yew grew by the ruined wall, sending its roots over and through the remaining stonework subsequent to the Dissolution. It's therefore old but hardly in the veteran league.

NOT TRUE !

Myths and legends are a fascinating aspect of our culture, whether featuring trees or not. From time to time a piece of fiction gets published as fact and is then repeated so often nobody doubts it. Back in 1958 the encumbent of Tandridge Parish Church was writing a new church guide book and described the way the builders of the Saxon church arched the masony of the foundations over the roots of the great yew tree so as not to damage them. It was a wonderful illustration of the reverence paid by our ancestors to such a tree and provided architectural evidence that testified to the Yew having been already massive back in Saxon times. It must date far back into pre-Christian times. This evidence is still much quoted today.

To see such arches implies a crypt but there is no crypt under Tandridge church, let alone a Saxon one. There have been occasions when the foundation layers below ground level have been exposed and still no arches have been found. The church is not even Saxon and there is no architectural, archaeological or documentary evidence for there ever having been one. The first church on the site is the present one, which was started in early Norman times - and the Normans didn't build arches over the roots either! The whole story is a fabrication.

Divided and hollow after more than two thousand years, the Yew at Tandridge is still defiantly sprouting from its base to grow on for more centuries yet.

Ewhurst is the only Surrey village to be named directly after Yew trees. When the Normans built their church here, in the early 12th century, they no doubt used an ancient sacred spot. The village of Ewell, sounding like another Yew tree connection is named after the springs or wells, and this seems so even when the Saxon name is traced back into the Celtic languages. Perhaps these were once Celtic 'Wells of Destiny'.

YEW

Taxus baccata L.

When the New Year sunshine catches the Downs to the east of Guildford, it's a rich brown quilting of trees on its chalk bed that glows warmly. It's enriched with an even patchwork of bottle-green Yew trees, right down to the fieldside fringes. It's best between the Silent Pool and Shere.

Up on the hill behind, at Newlands Corner, is one of Surrey's two ancient Yew groves. The other is in Norbury Park in the Mole valley below Dorking. They are national treasures and despite hurricane damage continue to defy time. Inevitably they get dubbed 'Druids' Groves' for which there is no archaeological evidence but on the other hand, tradition may be right. Some of the trees are old enough to have known the Celtic people who venerated the Yew.

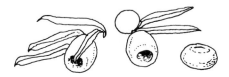

The trees were still respected as marking sacred sites when Christianity arrived, so the new churches were built right up against the trees to maintain a continuity of sacredness and impose the new religion. They are still there at places like Ashtead and Little Bookham. For the biggest and oldest, and the one with the longest documented history in Surrey, go to Crowhurst churchyard. The Yew is calculated to have been there some 4,000 years, making it fifth oldest in the country, and now has a trunk measuring 32 feet round. It's near the River Eden and the derivation of that name, from long before any knowledge of the Garden of Eden, is argued by some to indicate a very special place in ancient times.

Perhaps more impressive than the Crowhurst Yew is the one in Tandridge churchyard. This one, although perhaps only 2,000 years old, is of exceptional height. It probably gave its name to the place, for *tan* translates as *red* or sometimes *sacred*, so the Yew with its red bark and berries could be the tan on the ridge. If so, this could well be one of the cultural centres from before Saxon times, one of a group of places which must have existed but about which we know so little. Tandridge continues the tradition by giving its name to the present Borough.

In those pre-Saxon days, a prime location needed the three essential features of the cosmology of the time: a sacred tree of life connecting earth and sky, a hill, mound or crest to represent the Earth's Navel or the World Mountain, and, thirdly, a well or spring to represent the Well of Destiny. It could be argued that two of them are still recognisable at Tandridge.

For a Well of Destiny perhaps we should look at Dunsfold. The Yew there beside the church probably pre-dates Christianity and down the bank below it, beside the river, is one of only three holy wells in Surrey. Were people venerating its healing waters long before the coming of Christianity?

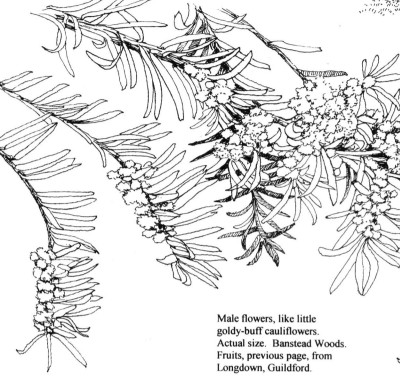

Male flowers, like little goldy-buff cauliflowers. Actual size. Banstead Woods. Fruits, previous page, from Longdown, Guildford.

One thing is certain: there are some grand old Yews around the county to stir our wonderings. There are about twenty of them, from Warlingham to Haslemere, Hambledon to Alfold. What cultural changes they have seen! Some still signal just that, like the one at Titsey where the church was destroyed in 1775 when a new park house was built. The Yew was left. It's about 1,000 years old and 21 feet round. It was retained for its ornamental value and the Yew tree served these ideals long before notions of the 'ornamental' became a national style. For example, in 1538, at the Dissolution of the Monasteries, Henry VIII had his gardeners retrieve the Yews from London's Charterhouse for a new home at Hampton Court Palace.

At the other end of the social scale I like the story told by Rev. F. W. Cobb about one of the earlier incumbents at remote Alfold. Rector Sparkes had eighteen children and the girls built a platform up in the top of a Yew tree from where, with the aid of a telescope, they spied on the poet Lord Tennyson walking his Aldworth estates miles away on Blackdown. Oh what fun those girls must have had scrambling up the tree, so far away from the critical eyes of those Victorian ladies who held views on the way young ladies should deport themselves!

The tree is very variable, giving rise to over a hundred cultivars and continued debate as to how many are distinct species. Thus there is a wealth of variety in the county. One of the commonest and most impressive is *Taxus baccata* 'Dovastoniana', the Westfelton Yew, which came to national notice about 1777. It's easily spotted for having little pendulous branchlets dangling from its spreading boughs. Come March these can be quite golden, from trapping so much of the pollen shed by all the tiny male cones nestling against the stems. Later, the female trees come into their own with their burden of brilliant red arils with their pinkish powdering of bloom across the flesh. Do not eat them. The seed inside is very poisonous.

BLACKTHORN or SLOE

Prunus spinosa L.

When the sky is a slate roof pressing a closeness of grey light upon the wintry earth, then the Blackthorn foams in its whiteness of blossom. All the time the coldness lasts then so do the blooms, waiting for mildness to bring the pollinating insects. The job done, the petals fall. So it is that

If it's cold when the Blackthorn bursts
It'll be cold till the petals fall.

Thus the folklore is observational rather than predictive. It means that the Blackthorn became the second significant tree of the year, after the demise of the Christmas tree and other decorations on 6th January. The next day the women returned to work, spinning off wool from their distaffs, on what became known as Distaff's Day. The men didn't return to work until the first Monday, known as Plough Monday. They had just a few weeks to complete all the ploughing and harrowing ready for the spring sowing and that was timed according to the Blackthorn:-

When the Blackthorn blossoms white
Sow your Barley day and night.
or
When the sloe tree is as white as a sheet
Sow your barley whether it's dry or wet.

Thus it settled in the soil while all was cold ready to sprout at the next mildness. The lore is right too. Spring Barley is traditionally sown in February and March, being far hardier than Wheat, and Blackthorn is usually fully blossoming by then. Some strains begin in January in mild years; 14th January in 1998. Other strains wait until the leaves are bursting and that could be a bit late for Barley so folklore gives 1st March as a deadline:-

Upon St. David's Day
Put Oats and Barley in the clay.

13

Gathering the sloes on a beautiful autumn day on the Downs lodges in many a memory today but go back to medieval Surrey and the chief use was for *trouse* or the spiny twiggy tops. These made medieval barbed wire. The twigs, all savage with cruel spines, were heaped around young trees or sprouting coppice stools to keep off grazing animals. They were used for plugging gaps in hedges too. This was overseen by the *hayward*, whose job it was to protect the hay meadows, by keeping out the animals. He patrolled stretches of hedge-cutting lest anyone commit the sin of leaving thorny twigs on the field edge. Medieval labourers worked barefoot!

These *spiney* suckering thickets were the original *spinneys* leaving a legacy in Surrey only as a word used indiscriminately. Haywards survive as surname. The tree is rather scattered nowadays but could serve more often that it does in the plantings beside main highways. The Mole valley north of Dorking, at Denbies, still has enough Blackthorn for it to be highlighted as a landscape feature in 1993 by the National Trust. On Box Hill opposite, in the same year, it was included by the Trust among 5,000 saplings used for restoring the landscape.

Do not pick the blossom. It has guardian spirits which will cause strife if it's brought indoors - a belief that goes back to the Celts and from them to the Ancient Greeks - Eris (Blackthorn) was a source of strife to her twin brother Ares (Hawthorn). Thus the two trees should not be grown together. Eris and Ares were born to Hera, wife of Zeus, after she had touched the Hawthorn pointed out to her by Flora. Thus the Christians adopted Hawthorn as a symbol of the miraculous conception. For this reason it was hated by the first Protestants but used by recusant Catholics to signal to each other. Bringing it indoors to signal through the roadside windows would indeed be dangerous if it caught the attention of those who would persecute a Catholic.

BOX

Buxus sempervirens L.

Overlapping the seasonal prominence of the Blackthorn was the Box. Sadly, little has been recorded of its cultural importance but it seems to have been significant at Candlemas, on 2nd February. That was a Christian update of the old Celtic fire festival of Imbolc, when the earth was purified, ready for a new year, and the men could then return to the plough.

The spiritual force to which they turned was Bride or Brigit or Brigid. Her role in purifying the earth for another season's crops was too vital for the earliest Christians to suppress, so they had to adopt her. Now she has 'saint' in front of her name. Her festival of cleansing was Christianised as the Feast of the Purification, commemorating the presentation of the eight-day-old Jesus to the Temple. That was when Simeon recognised the baby as the fresh hope for the future. Box was one of the prime plants for ritual decoration at this time, and remained so until at least the 19th century in Ireland where offerings of Box were still being taken to the sites dedicated to St. Brigid.

Ultimately Box had varying roles according to the region. In some places it was hung up with other evergreens as a symbolic way of carrying fertility over from one year to the next. That ritual was also adopted by the early Christians, as 'Christmas decorations,' sanctioned by Pope Gregory I in 604. He based his authority on a verse in the Book of Isaiah:-

"The glory of Lebanon shall come unto thee, the fir tree, the pine tree and the box together, to beautify the place of my sanctuary."

Alternatively, Box was omitted from the Christmas evergreens in regions where they stayed in place beyond Twelfth Night until the Eve of Candlemas. Then they were replaced by Box, which probably stayed in place until the beginning of Lent. More widespread was its use later in Lent on Palm Sunday. It is often said this was one of the substitutes to which the English turned when they couldn't afford the expensive import of true palm. However many churchwarden accounts record purchases of 'palm, yew and box' for 'garnishing' the church for Palm Sunday. This is a persistent trio, making it clear that Box was there in its own right. Such records of purchases are inevitably from towns, whereas out in the countryside the ritual plants were gathered and given free to the church - leaving us with a paucity of documentation! Presumably there was a good market for Surrey Box from all the London churches.

Another demand for Box, that lasted until the 19th century at least, was for funerals. It's an old favourite, found in Sussex graves of the Saxons, and is probably part of that notion of carrying life onwards, put in the grave to carry the life of the soul over from mortality to immortality. The tree certainly has a mysterious past, but it does give us something to ponder when walking the Downs around Box Hill. There the smooth green and black trunks, slowly and so very solidly, lift their dark canopies up among the other trees into the light.

This is a pleasure that has attracted visitors for hundreds of years - by the 17th century walks had been cut through the Box woods for this very enjoyment. When John Evelyn visited Sir Richard Stidolph at Norbury Park in 1655 he recorded in his diary the *"goodly walks and hills shaded with Yew and Box."* Later, Evelyn recorded in his *Silva,*(1662), *"the ladies, gentlemen, and other water-drinkers from the neighbouring Ebesham [Epsom] Spaw [Spa], often resort during the heat of summer to walk, collation and divert themselves in those antilex natural alleys, and shady recesses, among the Box trees..."* About 1694 that great traveller Celia Fiennes recorded, *"The hill is full of Box which is cutt out in severall walks, shady and pleasant to walk..."* Then in 1808 William Gilpin found *"shivering precipices, and downy hillocks, everywhere interspersed with the mellow verdure of box, which is here and there tinged, as box commonly is, with red and orange."* The list could go on, especially as the little village of Mickleham, sheltering beneath all this grandeur, attracted so many literary people in the 18th and 19th centuries. Through their letters and diaries we can enjoy their walks through the Box trees.

Sadly, today, the trees are no longer promoted as a tourist attraction, yet there are only five counties that have wild Box. The National Trust which safeguards Box Hill also holds one of the National Collections of the tree but far away in Suffolk. The other two National Collections are in Avon and Hampshire. Visitors to Dorking are given no inclination of this heritage - nor of the equally important Junipers - only the white Dorking chicken sits on the name boards.

JUNIPER

Juniperus communis L. ssp. communis

"Five and twenty ponies
Trotting through the dark -
Brandy for the parson,
'Baccy for the Clerk,
Laces for a lady, letters for a spy...."
(from Rudyard Kipling's "Smugglers Song")

Surrey was smugglers' country. It lay across their routes from the Channel coast to London and had deep secretive ways entrenched in the flanks of the central band of hills. Here it was difficult for the Excise men to know where to ambush next and their best intentions were often foiled by the locals who appreciated the smugglers. Through them they got their decent tea - the London stuff was often adulterated with dried Ash leaves to make it taste so foul that 'common' folk wouldn't develop a liking for it. The rich could pay. Brandy for the parson - is that why the table tombs in Cranleigh churchyard are said to have been used for storage? Laces for the ladies - oh yes, our flax, plentiful as it was, went for coarser wear. There was a proposal to start a lace-making school at Egham but nothing seems to have come of it. High-class linen was produced at Ockley but that seems to have been sold on. Smugglers satisfied market demands, just as they do still!

Many of those old routes into the hills are still referred to as smugglers' tracks today. Otherwise the landscape has changed dramatically, with woodland spreading over the old sheep pastures and shading out the thickets of brambles, Hawthorn, Blackthorn and Juniper. These, all armed with spines and prickles and thorns, are where the smugglers hid their contraband during the daylight hours.
"An old shepherd who worked on the chalk downs a few miles to the north, who was eighty two years of age in 1889, told how smugglers used to bring their pack-loads of brandy up Combe Bottom and hide them among the thickets of juniper, thorn and bramble."
(Gertrude Jekyll, *Old West Surrey*, 1904)

In particular, it's the prickly Junipers, or 'jinnipers' as they were called in Surrey, that have become so rare. Before the First World War, when F. E. Green was preparing *The Surrey Hills* (pub. 1915) he was able to observe that he knew *"the chalk downs by the short grass, by the sight of the yew, the juniper, and the beech."* Now they seem to be extinct upon the sandstone hills, although they lasted until the Second World War in places like Peaslake. That just leaves a few on the chalk - on Epsom Downs beyond the racecourse towards Tadworth, and some more above the Brockham quarry. Otherwise their last great Surrey stronghold is on Box Hill. Sometimes they grow with a spreading habit which must have been excellent for concealing contraband. Others grew as beautiful blue-green columns like Cypress trees to put a hint of Tuscany on the Surrey hills.

Junipers have declined for a whole combination of reasons. Certainly the tree has been over-harvested for raw materials and been stripped of its seed-bearing fruits to flavour gin and beer, but, it will also have had its ups and downs in relation to shifts in the climate; it does best under continental conditions and poorly when the British climate is at its most maritime. This shows up well on the Continent where Juniper replaces Gorse on the heaths as Gorse prefers maritime conditions. Other biological factors are important too. Natural regeneration is very slow because the fruits develop over two or three years before the seed is viable. Then they only germinate well after a fire. Changes in land management means winter grass is now rarely burnt off to encourage fresh growth for the sheep because the sheep have gone. Trees have taken over but Junipers hate shade and being dripped on.

These are the last precious relics of the great Juniper woods of 12,000 years ago. It's time we took a pride in them and planted some more.

THE SMUGGLERS' SYSTEM
Contraband was moved by night and concealed for the daylight hours with the compliance of the locals. These would visit the hiding places after a 'run' and put a mark on some of the hoard to indicate the price of their silence and protection. These goods were left behind the next night. Some were needed to reward officials, like the Justice of the Peace, for being 'slack' in their duty. Newcomers to the system, with a 'misdirected' sense of duty, who might not be fully aware of the importance of this 'trade' in the local economy, were soon persuaded of the fact when the locals refused to co-operate with work, deliveries, etc.

16

All in all, the Cedar was welcomed into England by both the Church and the country landowners for their parks. Many a Surrey churchyard has a Cedar, from Tilford to Christ Church, Esher, just as the parks are similarly adorned, from Gatton, Painshill, Peper Harow, and Woburn to Claremont Landscape Garden.

The Claremont Cedars by the lake were so scenic that they have been much used for book illustration. It has been a matter of debate as to whether these were planted by Capability Brown as part of his work at Claremont - a debate that was settled by the Great Storm of 1987 which brought one down and enabled the annual rings to be counted. Despite its size it was not as old as people thought, dating only from 1801.

CEDAR OF LEBANON

Cedrus libani A. Rich.

In 1846 a Cedar seedling was planted in the churchyard at Cranleigh by the rector, Archdeacon John Henry Saptre, (sketched above and unusual for having lost its leader and become multi-trunked). This one came from Lebanon itself where the Cedars once grew in great forests up the mountains (being replanted today) where Solomon sent 30,000 Israelites from the army, followed by 150,000 soldiers and 3,300 officers, to bring down the Cedars for building the great Temple in Jerusalem. They took them down to the sea and floated the trunks south, lashed together in great rafts, to near present-day Tel Aviv from where they were carried inland to Jerusalem. It took seven years but at 40m high and with trunks up to 9m in diameter, these were the greatest trees known to the people. Cedar wood had long been highly desirable, being a sign of status, wealth and power. When it came to crucifying Christ it was said that the block of wood upon which Christ stood was of Cedar and for rendering this service the Cedar has been accepted into Christianity.

The Great Storm also took out two of the group of Cedars in the manor grounds, up beside the tower of Compton church (boxed sketch, 1987). These again have been much used for book illustration, being some of the largest and finest in England, and the ring count of the casualty provided a date of c.1750. What caused more comment though, was the way the wind managed to bring down two in different directions, one on either side of the church. Was that divine intervention or a convolution of wind eddies?

Cholera must have been a very frightening disease when it broke out in Elstead. The survivors gathered in church for a service of thanksgiving for their deliverance, and made a collection from which they bought Lime trees for the churchyard and a Cedar of Lebanon. These were planted in November 1849 and now that Cedar is massive, sending down great sweeping boughs to dust off the headstones - a rare sight in a county where most of the mature Cedars have been shorn of their lower boughs. With these so low it is possible to get a close view of the beautiful cones or 'clogs' as they used to be called, sitting in rows like baby owls.

18

Elstead 1985

MAGNOLIAS
Magnolia spp. and hybrids

While the English countryside plays a tentative fanfare for spring with a flurry of catkins on Alder and Pussy Willow, our gardens raise a toast to the sun in glorious goblets of white and rose and claret-purple. It's Magnolia time again. If the frosts keep off, the celebration will last for a couple of weeks.

The genus of some 125 spp. has the largest flowers of any garden tree or shrub and the largest of the spring flowerers is *Magnolia x soulangiana*. It's a garden invention, created by, and named after, the French gardener Etienne Soulange-Bodin (1774-1846). He crossed *Magnolia denudata* with *Magnolia liliflora* and waited. In 1826 the first sapling flowered. The first English description was by John Lindley for the *Botanical Register* in 1828. He had to work from a drawing, made at the Epsom Nursery of Messrs. Charles, James and Peter Young. They had one of the most extensive collections of rare plants in the country and when it came to *Magnolia x soulangiana* they simply bought up the entire stock from M. Soulange-Bodin for 500 guineas - "in consequence of which that fine tree will be spread over the country," reported J. C. Loudon. How right he was. It's now the most popular of all Magnolias and is also the most adaptable. While purists want it planted in moist humus-rich soils in a woodland setting where it can grow up to thirty feet between the trees, the weekend gardener bungs it in the front garden and hopes for the best. It grows! It may be short and shrubby but it grows and the older it gets the better it flowers.

Travellers around the county come across pockets of enthusiasm for it, suggesting it had been a speciality of a local nursery. Such is the Rowtown/Liberty Lane area of Addlestone, adjoining the former grounds of the Fletcher family's 'Ottershaw Nursery' (origin of *Chamaecyparis lawsoniana* 'Fletcheri'). Whether that nursery inspired so many plantings isn't known. Their plant lists for the 1920s offer only "Magnolias in variety" but they are hardly likely to have turned their backs on the best of the spring salutations.

Top ~ Chertsey Rd. Chobham 9

ALDER

Alnus glutinosa (L.) Gaertner

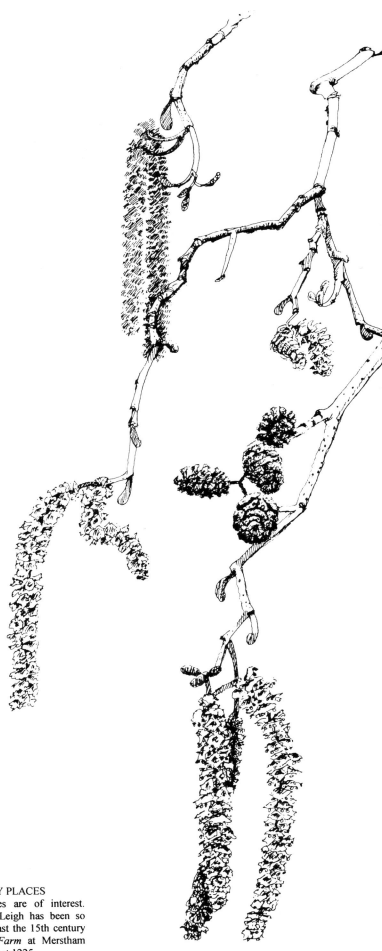

Once the Hazels have laced the hedgerows with their golden glory of coming spring, it's the Alders that join in. Their catkins are one of the unsung beauties of the countryside - they often look dark maroon from a distance but turn one up in the palm of your hand and you'll find rich crimson under the scales and there the anthers nestle as brilliant golden beads. Other species with longer and more golden catkins are being introduced as street trees, as they do not have very widely spreading branches. These include *Alnus cordata*, the Italian Alder from southern Italy and Corsica (Burys Car park, Godalming), and *Alnus incana*, the Grey Alder from the Caucasus (Epsom streets).

If we could go back and visit any of the gunpowder mills in Surrey, such as Chilworth, then we'd find the Alder fulfilling two important functions. It's one of the main ingredients of gunpowder, after the timber has been converted into charcoal. Secondly, we wouldn't be allowed to wear traditional hob-nailed boots in case we kicked up a spark - not a good idea in a gunpowder works! Instead, workers wore clogs and for these Alder wood was deemed best. It's easy to shape, doesn't split in use, withstands wetting, is light to wear, doesn't put splinters in your feet and feels warm. Even after the advent of rubber-soled boots the clogs persisted in some workplaces, such as breweries and timber yards, until after the Second World War. They were still being offered for sale in Guildford until the end of the 1940s/early 1950s. Modern British fashion clogs are still made from Alder.

Clogs are difficult to find in old photographs because the footwear disappears into the shadows under the seat. You can almost hear those early photographers saying, "tuck your feet in!" Then there is a problem over distinguishing clogs from hob-nailed boots because British clogs have the leather uppers taken down over the wood and nailed close to the ground, making them look like boots. The tell-tale row of nail heads is often difficult to spot. The best sources, to get feet in full light, are workers up ladders, such as fruit pickers and thatchers.

SURREY PLACES
Two place names are of interest. *Nalderswood* at Leigh has been so called since at least the 15th century and *Alderstead Farm* at Merstham goes back to at least 1225.

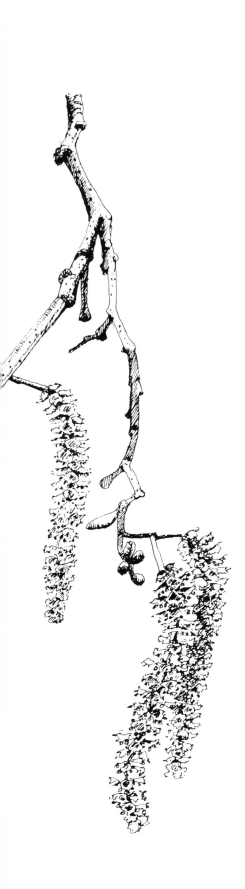

CHANGING TIMES
One of the last
village cobblers.
Recorded 1991
at Ripley.

Tracing the makers of the clogs is even more difficult because two craftsmen were involved: cloggers and cobblers. Firstly, cloggers cut and roughly shaped the wood on the riverbank according to need and opportunity. This seems to have been largely a sideline of people who get lumped in the census returns as agricultural labourers. Their work was no doubt intermittent and seasonal, just another in the range of skills practised by country people. Their work was sold on for finishing and sale by cobblers where clogs become indistinguishable from other types of footwear. Even for high fashion shoes the Alder had its uses, primarily for wooden heels.

Alders are a generous renewable resource because once felled they shoot from the stump. The last crop of shoots at the decline of the tree's usefulness have now grown on into multi-trunked trees. These are so familiar over much of Surrey that it's difficult to find old single-trunked specimens. At Abinger Hammer there's a grand double trunked one, with a massive girth at the base. It's in the meadow beside the Tillingbourne in the centre of Abinger Hammer.

In Surrey there always seems to have been enough Alder to satisfy demand but elsewhere Birch had to be used as well. On the Continent, Beech was preferred, since freshly cut Alder exudes orange-red sap, resembling bleeding, which was taken as an ill omen, or worse still, was said to be the blood of Christ. In Surrey, such beliefs and any of greater antiquity, seem to have died out at an early date and did not interfere with its usage. The only folklore arises from the tree's love of wet places which gave it an association with water sprites etc. Rather than being a true belief, this was probably a way of deterring children from playing in dangerous places like riverbanks. The notion that Alder is unlucky is primarily Irish and seems to have come into Surrey in the 19th century with railway navvies and immigrants following the potato famine.

PUSSY WILLOW

Salix caprea L and similar species and hybrids

When the Alders are in catkin so the silver faces of the Pussy Willows doff their dark brown hats. Soon they're as golden as the cheering sun. Armfuls of twigs were carried off to churches for the Palm Sunday service, as a substitute for the true Palm which was otherwise an expensive import. Some came in with returning pilgrims (palmers) to prove they'd reached the Holy Land. On Palm Sunday the sprays were blessed and then processed around the church and churchyard to the south door. The Holy Sacrament was taken along too, under a special canopy. Then at the door, sometimes from special scaffolding there, boys sang the *Gloria Laus* before the people were showered with flowers and cakes. No doubt Surrey found a ready market for Pussy Willow with the London churches. Thus the churchwardens' accounts include such entries as:-

"for palme flowers and cake against palme Sunday.....iiijd"
(St. Margaret Pattens, 1524)
"for Palme flowers and cakes on Palme Sunday.....vd"
(St. Mary Woolnoth, 1539)

Willows for rejoicing were also ordained in the translation of the King James Bible (not in the modern Good News Bible) wherein it says:
And ye shall take you on the first day the boughs of goodly trees, branches of palm trees, and the boughs of thick trees, and willows of the brook; and ye shall rejoice before the Lord your God seven days.
(Leviticus 23, 40)

There are many beautiful Willows in Britain but nothing to beat sprays of Pussy Willow when the fluffy gold catkins straggle along the branch like a gaggle of goslings. That was once a familiar image, when so many people kept geese ('Poor Man's Beef') and looked forward to Christmas. In those days the catkin sprays were known by some sort of goose name such as Goslings or Goose-and-Goslings, since the name Pussy Willow is not traditional. It came from America in the mid 19th century.

Top - Little Bookham Church, which, like Surrey's other ancient churches would have seen the Pussy Willow rituals for Palm Sunday. The sketch also shows the ancient Yew, while round on the north side of the churchyard can be found a Weeping Ash and a Weeping Holly.

23

WORKING WILLOWS

Salix viminalis L.
Salix fragilis L.
and others

In 1767 Gilbert White recalled in one of his letters for *The Natural History of Selborne* a visit he had made some ten years earlier to the Sunbury home of his friend Rev. John Muslo. He'd looked out onto the Osier beds beside the Thames when great flocks of Swallows were gathering there. He pondered whether or not they migrated, or whether they hibernated underwater, which was a Swedish theory of the time. Only one or two Osiers survive there today but formerly this stretch of the Thames was one of the five great basket-making centres in Britain.

They used a variety of species, not just the 'true' Osier, *Salix viminalis*, growing in the riverside mudflats. In those days the Thames was tidal right up to Walton Bridge. That ended in the 19th century, with the construction of locks, such as Teddington. Then the mudflats dried out and started sprouting villas. Some willow beds survived in use until well into the 20th century. Those at Penton Hook were bought off the Lord of the Manor, Lord Lucan, in 1923 by the Harris family, who used their boatyard for stripping and bundling the wands. Then they were punted across the Thames to Laleham where there was a wharf at the end of Vicarage Lane. From there they went on to the London furniture-makers. The last baskets are said to have been made by the furnishers, F. Lewis, in Staines High Street, during the Second World War, for parachuting medical supplies into Arnhem.

It's rarely clear in the old writings which willows are being recorded. The Saxons set the pattern for later usage with *seale* (sallow), usually for bushy species and *wilig* (willow) for the more tree-like species. *Osier* is of French origin and came in during the Middle Ages. *Withes* and *withies* were usually the wands and not necessarily of willow. Thus, going back to Walton-on-Thames, we find the land by the bridgehead called Cowey Sale, which is believed to derive from *seale*.

Male catkins of Pussy Willow.
Unlike many other catkins these
have nectaries to attract pollinating
insects as well as having masses of
pollen for wind pollination.
Esher Common, 1997.

Osier catkins - Sunbury-on-Thames

The village of Seale in the Wey Valley by Farnham preserves its Saxon spelling but why call a place after willow trees when there were miles and miles of them right down the valley? The Wey was prone to flooding which must have promoted thousands of willows. There must have been a significance of some sort. Since the Willow was the ancient tree of death perhaps this is where the local pagan Saxon tribe held its funeral rites. Maybe Seale was originally an important basket-making centre? We'll never know. Salfords, meaning the ford by the Willows, is an easier village name to understand.

Only occasionally were the trunks used for timber, notably for cricket bats from the Cricket Bat Willow, *Salix alba var. caerulea.* That's an Essex story but in Surrey three of them have been planted by Abinger Sports Club beside their playing field. Otherwise, willows were grown as pollards so that the flush of shoots could be cropped regularly - the 'lop-and-top' system employed by Overseers of the Poor to provide cheap fuel. Shoots left to grow into stouter poles, together with the timber, had at least seventy nine different uses - these really were working willows!

Uses included innumerable types of basket for all manner of tasks, which have now become redundant or supplanted by modern materials. The medieval backpack (woven from willow) or *ped* is perpetuated in the name of its user - a pedlar.

Ancient hollow
Willow pollards.
Beside the pond on
North Holmwood village green
1993

25

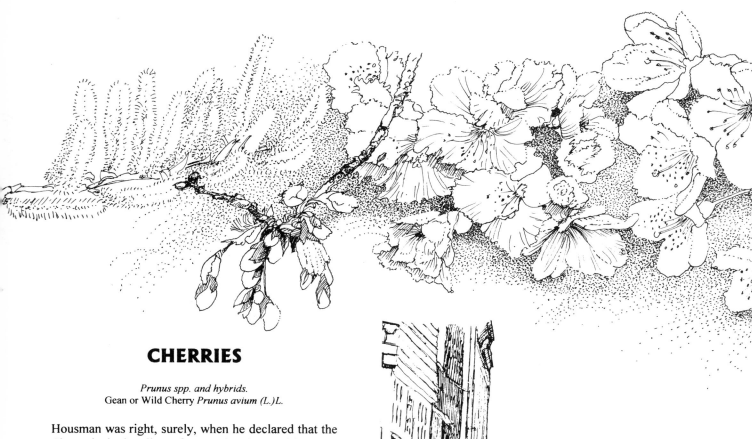

CHERRIES

Prunus spp. and hybrids.
Gean or Wild Cherry *Prunus avium (L.)L.*

Housman was right, surely, when he declared that the Cherry is the loveliest of trees when hung with bloom along the bough. With introduced species and new hybrids it's possible to have one in blossom throughout the winter and right through to the end of spring. Best of all, though, is surely when the wild Gean whitens the dark woods just before the main flush of new green. They are always grand on the downs, perhaps because the hillside tiers them up one above the other ready to enjoy that drama of unfurling greenery. There are lovely stands on the hills behind Godstone, new plantings by the Sheepleas's ranger following the Great Storm of 1987, and plenty in the woods and hedgerows around Dorking where they supported a local wine industry in the 18th century, *"There is a kind of wild Black Cherry, that grows about Dorking, of which the inhabitants make considerable quantities of red wine, much wholesomer and but little inferior to French Claret."*

(1750; A New Present State of England)

June was cherry-picking time and they were in great demand. The Tudors had been particularly keen on them. Indeed, Evelyn claims it was Henry VIII who introduced Cherry orchards into England which, if true, must refer to commercial orchards as there are plenty of royal and monastic references to indicate that Cherries were popular and grown widely in the Middle Ages. By 1600 they cost 8d a pound when a day's labour cost 6d. In 1618 the chaplain to the Venetian Ambassador in London observed: *"The numerous sorts of cherries and egriots [sour cherries] which one sees in Italy may well be desired in this kingdom, though certainly not enjoyed, for generally in the markets they sell one single sort of very bad morella. Yet the English are extremely greedy of them, especially the women, buying them at the beginning of the season in bunches at the cost of an eye."* *(Galinou, p.82)*

26

Coincidentally, it has been Dorking people who have sent in reminders of *The Cherry-Tree Carol*. It used to be very popular throughout much of Christendom but has largely fallen from favour today. It tells how the Virgin Mary, heavy with child, was wandering through a Cherry orchard with Joseph whom she asked to stretch up and pick her a cherry. The testy old man retorted:

Let him pluck thee a cherry
that brought thee with child.

Miraculously the tree bent over and delivered cherries unto Mary. These were the only fruits fit for the Virgin in England, whereas French and Spanish versions have apples, while Middle Eastern ones feature a Palm tree. They all derive from the unauthorised stories of Christ's childhood in the apocryphal gospels. Thus some versions are set later, after the birth of Jesus, on the third day of The Flight Into Egypt, which sets it in January when there are no cherries. Fear not, extra verses provide us with a miraculous flush of early blossom and very rapid fruiting! Some versions have more miracles than others but the point of all of them, in their later verses, is the foretelling of Christ's death. Sadly, to have Joseph speaking "with words most unkind" was more than the Victorians could cope with so you won't hear it sung in the pubs of Dorking today.

(four texts and variations can be found in Child)

Selling fruit and dairy produce to London enabled the Mole Valley people to survive hard times following bad corn harvests. Cherries were always an important harvest, not just for fresh fruit but also as an ingredient of liqueurs (kirsch) and, under their country name of mazard, for flavouring brandy (brandy mazard). All parts of the tree have been used including dried fruit stalks for mild diarrhoea, the bark for cough syrup and the fruit stones for charcoal in gas masks, as at Ewell, where in July 1918 the Rural District Council made arrangements for collecting fruit stones and nut shells for gas mask charcoal. The timber is still prized by cabinet makers.

All this abundance of fruit will astonish growers today who find their trees plagued by birds. Although some birds were far rarer in the past, like starlings, we are probably reading testimonies to the efficiency of the local children with their slingshots. Small birds were 2d a dozen in Tudor markets and for long afterwards - *"Four and twenty blackbirds baked in a pie..."* is not just a nursery rhyme. Many were trapped in birdlime, made from Holly bark. Otherwise they had to be scared off - a crafty farmer at Alfold took the school bell when it became redundant and set it up among his cherries with a long string trailing to his back door!

Among the blossom of wild and fruiting Cherries there are numerous cultivars grown specifically for their blossom. These are the so-called Japanese Cherries, although not all of them originated in Japan or from wild Japanese species. They haven't been here very long. The first significant introductions came in 1822 but it wasn't until the next century that they became so popular - when the notion of the 'Garden City' had diluted down to 1930s street plantings. Many a ribbon development was paralleled with avenues of Japanese Cherries or Horse Chestnuts, neither of which respond well to hard pruning when their branches started smacking traffic. Nevertheless, many people grew up with the idea that a Japanese Cherry is one smothered with frilly double pink icing-sugar blossom. That's due to 'Kanzan' which became available about 1913 and rapidly became one of the most popular of all.

The pretty little church at Buckland that is such a landscape feature when driving east up the A25 became a real eye-catcher when floating in its pink froth of the surrounding Cherries. These had to be felled but, thankfully, have been replaced to cheer future years. Visit Cranleigh church at pink-time too. Since a bomb took out the coloured glass in the Second World War the big east window has been glazed with clear but rippled glass, through which there's a wonderful pink cherry blur. It's become significant too, since the Cherry trees in Hiroshima somehow survived the atomic bomb and later sprouted blossom from their blackened limbs so that now the Japanese Cherry has been adopted as a symbol of the Resurrection. There are some at the Cathedral on Stag Hill but a whole collection of Surrey cultivars could be planted there, to create a greater avenue of praise. The most glorious avenue is across Cobham Tilt on the way to Stoke D'Abernon, whether you drive through it or turn off to view it from the southern green, preferably against a black storming sky. For those who prefer a more natural show of pink and white try the rear churchyard at Horsell.

Top - Old Dorking backs,
by King's Arms 1988

WELLINGTONIA

Sequoiadendron giganteum (Lindley) Buchholz

The very hallmark of an old Surrey garden or estate is a mature Wellingtonia, or, better still, an avenue of them. Their sudden popularity is rather surprising considering nobody in Britain had seen one, it having "remained unknown to the civilized world till the spring of 1852, when it was accidentally discovered by a hunter [A. T. Dowd], in the employ of the Union Water Company of California, whose duty it was to supply the Company's men with fresh meat." This was part of the Californian Gold Rush and that of course was particularly newsworthy.

The discovery of the trees was reported widely and wildly. Exaggerated figures for height, girth and age were gossiped round the world until the United States government released official figures, declaring the tallest to be 325 feet. It made little difference. It could grow as tall as the spire of Salisbury Cathedral and who could turn away from having such a landmark on their estates? Not many in Surrey apparently!

They were all planted on the strength of the reports. Landowners hadn't *seen* a mature specimen. There were no pictures in the catalogues. Even in 1881 when James Veitch and Sons, of the famous Veitch nurseries in Exeter and Chelsea, published their *Manual of the Coniferae,* they only showed a coned branchlet and a couple of details. They were able to publish beautiful illustrations of other conifers and we might expect the same for a Wellingtonia since, as they pointed out in the text, the tree was brought to Britain by their own collector, William Lobb, in 1853. In fact James Veitch didn't think it had any beauty and said so, in the *Manual*:- "gigantic, ponderous, and imposing, but it cannot be called beautiful." (p.204)

Top - one branch-end in March 1998 showing the thick encrustation of little male cones, golden with pollen. There must have been so many millions of them in the mile-long avenue at Heatherside, shedding tonnes and tonnes of pollen in great golden clouds.

Right - one of the tallest of the Dartnell trees. To its left can be found one which, unusually, has a divided upper trunk.

American Big Trees remained in the news because Britain then had a row with America over choosing an English name. In the Sierra Nevada of California the local Mono peoples called it Woh-Woh-Nau in imitation of the call of the owl which they believed was the tree's guardian spirit. Once the tree arrived at Veitch's Exeter nursery in December 1853 Dr. John Lindley, of Royal Horticultural Society fame, wrote the first description of it, for the readers of the *Gardeners Chronicle* in the issue of 23rd December. Therein he named the tree *Wellingtonia gigantea* after the Duke of Wellington who had died the previous year. The French objected. The Americans were outraged. If it was going to have a patriotic name it was going to be Washingtonia after George Washington. They duly tried to establish the botanical names *Taxodium washingtonianum* and *Washingtonia californica*, which of course upset the British! The Americans argued that Washington liked trees, which was more than was said of Wellington! Then Queen Victoria apparently expressed a view favouring Wellington and that was that! At least, it was in 1938, when the argument was finally concluded with *Sequoiadendron giganteum*. Some claim this is the longest running botanical argument of its kind. *Sequoia* comes from the Cherokee name Sequoyah given to the son of a Cherokee woman who married an English trader. We can only write the name because it was that son (known in English as George Guess) who devised a way of writing down the Cherokee language, using eighty-six characters to represent the syllables. With the rest of his people he was driven out of his homelands and died in New Mexico in 1843.

During the second half of the 19th century the nurseries around Woking became the most important in the world and their vast range of trees and shrubs included this new American giant. Consequently there are many grand specimens around that district, of which the finest is reckoned to be the one at the bottom of St. John's Hill. The remains of an avenue survives at Dartnell Park, West Byfleet, where it now dwarfs the stream of traffic fuming along the busy A245.

About the only reward for being on the top of the multi-storey car parks in Woking is the long file of Wellingtonias marching along the western skyline before the high ground drops down into Camberley. In fact this avenue is over a mile long, making it not only the grandest treescape in Surrey but one of the most important in the country. It was back in 1850 that thirty acres were bought by a nurseryman from Forest Hill in Kent. He was Augustus Mongredien, born in Switzerland in 1806. Here at Heatherside he started a nursery that would ultimately cover over 300 acres, for the growing of over 500 different trees and shrubs. These were made more widely known in his book *Trees and Shrubs for English Plantations* (1870) in which he records "an avenue of Wellingtonias one mile in length but all too lately planted to afford any interest at present except to a botanist." If only he could see it now, for despite the various fortunes of the nursery and the modern housing developments of Heatherside, his avenue survives. Highways pass through it and along it, parts are reserved for walkers, closes of houses snuggle in underneath, footballers play beside it but it allows nothing to detract from the

Pyrford Church 1981

magnitude of its presence. It was planted for Mongedrien by Frederick Street in 1865. The Street family eventually took over the nursery and it stayed with them until 1922. Sadly, few saplings get planted nowadays, ready to replace the mature ones. They are very much part of Woking's heritage and fortunately that is the home of Martin Humphrey, Chairman of the Surrey branch of The International Tree Foundation and he has been instrumental in trying to perpetuate the trees of local importance. He has planted many personally and encouraged others, such as Knaphill's blacksmith who planted a Wellingtonia outside his smithy at the bottom of Anchor Hill in 1981. The smithy has now closed but the tree is growing on finely. The Borough Council has been persuaded of the value of this aspect of the local heritage and it now features in the Local Development Plan.

PEARS

*Pyrus pyraster (L) Burgsd
and Pyrus communis L.*

Pyrford, Pirbright, and Parley at Horsell are among the Surrey places named after pear trees. They are first recorded over a thousand years ago, in 10th century documents but how long before that they first evolved their names will never be known. What is intriguing is why pear trees should have been chosen at all. The trees of those days were of the Wild Pear, *Pyrus pyraster* which is very different from the fruit trees of today. The timber is extremely hard, making it difficult to work, and is so dense it barely floats. The fruits are rock hard and do not soften even after bletting by frosts. This is not exactly a very useful tree.

There isn't even agreement as to whether it is a native. Many think it was introduced from its other homeland in the Caucasus and Turkestan. That raises the question as to why something so useless should have been introduced at all. The answer to that is probably religious. Taking clues from overseas it might be that the fruits were fermented to brew a very alcoholic perry which was used for intoxication by the priests in order to commune with the gods. Being held sacred, even if only by tradition in later times, would deter people from felling it and that would explain its popularity as a boundary marker - it ranks fourth, nationally, in Anglo-Saxon charters. Cheats can move rocks but trees remain rooted to the spot.

This would add credence to the suspicion that Pyrford (meaning the ford at the pear trees) was an early religious site. In support of this, there is a rock which some think was a pre-Christian 'standing stone' and has been sanctified since with a Christian cross. This is not very convincing, for it stands only about knee-high and could just as likely have been a parish boundary marker. It is now planted in the grass at the entrance to Pyrford Court. Maybe the *ford* part of the name is significant too, for there is also a Perry Bridge at Shalford (recorded 1279). Perhaps there is an association with water deities, such as Bla. Christians continued to respect and fear the powers of water, building chapels on bridges and at fords for prayers and thanks for safe crossings, such as those to St. Martha and St. Catherine either side of the Wey crossing at Guildford.

Another contentious suggestion arises with Parley at Horsell which means the clearing in the pear tree wood. There is no evidence that Wild Pears grew as woods. As a species it occurs scattered through others. Possibly the Parley Pears were planted deliberately as one of those early sacred groves. Then early Christians cleared the trees in defiance of the old faith.

Pirbright, meaning the pear tree wood, could have the same significance. The religious usage would explain why the Wild Pear was apparently commoner and better known than it is today. Now there isn't even one recorded growing wild in Surrey.

It's certainly a very rare tree in Britain but there is also immense difficulty distinguishing it from degenerate Domestic Pears *(Pyrus communis)* that have sprung up from discarded cores. Domestic Pears are hybrids between several Wild Pear species and this genetic mix has given rise to the natural variation from which selections have been made to give so many different cultivars in later times. Thus references to pears from later medieval documents could, and probably do, refer to Domestic Pears. Pyrcroft at Chertsey, meaning the field with the pear tree, was not recorded until 1452 and is presumed to refer to a Domestic Pear but could, presumably, just as easily refer to an ancient Wild Pear that was still being treated with respect.

Pears were also adopted into the evolution of personal names. Thus the Horsley lands of Lower Pereyers derive their name from an early owner dubbed William atte Perie. We can only ponder what his connection was with the tree. We'll never understand the early story of pear trees but each spring there is a short flourish of brilliant white blossom to ensure we don't overlook them altogether.

PINES

Scots Pine - *Pinus sylvestris* L.
Corsican Pine - *Pinus nigra ssp. laricio* Maire

The scent of the pines on the heaths around Camberley is what helped to expand the tiny township of Victorian Camberley. It was deemed good for those fighting consumption (TB) and so in 1873 no less a publication than *The Lancet* was extolling the virtues of Camberley air. In 1899 the Brompton Hospital chose Camberley for the location of its country sanatorium, and estate agents were quick to promote Camberley as *the rising residential health resort.*

The same was happening at Hindhead. Here came to live Professor Tyndall, the scientist ranked second after Michael Faraday, and he declared the scent of the pines on the heath promoted good health just as much as that of the Alps. People changed from a Swiss health cure to building a villa in the Hindhead / Haslemere hills. How odd to think that the late Victorian developments of these two locations owe so much to the smell of a tree! - with a bit of help from the railways of course.

In 1759 a new but very similar species came to join it. This was the Corsican Pine, distinguished by not having the red upper trunk. Today it is very common in the county. They grow together at Abinger Roughs since a short December Saturday afternoon in 1989 when, with due ceremony, the National Trust initiated the planting of a small wood of 200 trees. They were paid for by public subscription as a memorial to the late Geoff Wharburton, council member of the Youth Hostel Association and a

Esher Common

Corsican Pines. Oxshott

The particular pines of these places were the Scots Pine; those trees with dark rugged bark below and rich orange brown above - the 'burnt sienna' of an artist's palette. For most of historic time in Surrey the tree had been absent but returns to the records in the 17th century, for which occurrence John Evelyn is often credited (or accused!). The 'evidence' for this is not very convincing. Even less so, is the story that it was planted in the Royal Park of Woking by its Keeper, Sir Edward Zouch, as a personal tribute to his Scottish master, King James I. It is to be doubted that the tree had ever disappeared completely and its rapid colonisation of the heaths was probably due to changes in land management but the question has yet to be answered convincingly.

life-long supporter of the National Trust. Many people have been commemorated by trees in Surrey but a whole wood is a rare compliment. This one, according to the Trust's press release, will "create an ideal focal point from the North Downs, Leith Hill and surrounding areas."

Nowadays there is far less scope for planting such focal points but prominent *clumps* were formerly a major feature in landscape design. Beeches were preferred on chalk and Pines on the sands. The great approach avenue to Chobham Place had both - an inner avenue of Beech and an outer avenue of Scots Pine, many of which survive and are part of the restoration programme being worked by the Borough of Surrey Heath. Young Scots Pines have now been interplanted between the veterans.

The native Scots Pine was complemented by the introduction (before 1596) of the Maritime Pine, *Pinus pinaster*, from the Mediterranean. It was included in the 18th century plantings at Claremont and has naturalised on several Surrey heaths, notably Blackheath where it's been recorded since 1893. Of the many new introductions that came from the American colonies, came one that was intended primarily to satisfy our need for ship masts. That was the lofty *Pinus strobus*, introduced in 1705, by Lord Weymouth - hence Weymouth Pine (and the French Pin du Lord). It was much promoted during the reign of Queen Anne but proved too susceptible to our species of aphids and rusts and is now used rarely for forestry. A young one can be seen in the Windlesham Arboretum but it has naturalised successfully in a few places in the west of the county, notably at Longcross where hundreds of plants were recorded in 1980.

building the multi-storey car park in Oriental Road the Borough Council accepted a design that was more individual than usual, with a hint of the Oriental, in keeping with the local heritage of Oriental Road. That produced great gusts of hot air. Now the fuss has died down and the pines are growing up. They are Monterey Pines *(Pinus radiata)*, introduced in 1833 from California, and planted here by Martin Humphrey (see Wellingtonias) to complement the style of the building, as they gradually develop their great domed heads. An added interest will

Just as these great trees confer 'architectural' form and scale to parkland so well-chosen species can work just as successfully in urban landscapes - softening harsh shapes and surfaces of concrete and brick while at the same time seeming to reduce the buildings to a more 'human' scale. Pines are worth greater consideration in these contexts, especially as their branches and roots are less spreading than many broad-leaved trees, allowing them to squeeze into narrow views most effectively. Thus in Surrey's most concrete of town centres, Woking, pines have been planted beside one of the more controversial buildings. When it came to

be their clusters of cones which grow permanently along the branches. They don't need to fall off as they are designed to burst open and shed their seeds after intense heating in a forest fire. Thus the usual advice for getting seed is to cut off the cones and bake them in an oven but Martin Humphrey reports a simpler way is to put them in a plastic bag and leave them on the car dashboard with the full force of the sun on them. With the fiery summers of late that is quite sufficient!

In New Zealand they are grown for paper pulp and make up the world's largest man-made forest. The seeds were sown by throwing them out of an aircraft.

HAWTHORN

Crayaegus monogyna Jacq.
Crataegus laevigata (Poiret) DC.

Just as the Blackthorn blossom opens the door to spring so the Hawthorn or May blossom flings wide the windows on summer. In May, Ranmore Common *"was redolent with Hawthorn. Indeed, the scent along the springy bridle path was almost overpowering,"* noted F. E. Green in 1915. A few years earlier Moul and Thompson had described Loseley as *"one of those stately ancestral parks, full of sweeping lawns, whitethorn brakes, and venerable trees, such as England alone can show."* They also quoted Edna Lyall remembering Farnham Park where there *"were Hawthorn trees to be climbed - one memorable one very near the castle was large enough to accommodate the whole cousinhood, five Brightonians and seven Farnham cousins."* That couldn't have been very comfortable since even the thick boughs are prone to retain their thorns! Never mind, the important thing is remembering - the spirit of the thorn tree listens to what we promise and ensures that we fulfil it.

We may think that listening notion was just a funny old wives' tale but it became embedded in the legal and local administrative systems. Oaths had to be sworn under particularly venerated thorns before they were replaced by the Bible, and the men of the Hundred met under such trees. At least twelve survive today according to Oliver Rackham but both examples in Surrey have been cut down in recent times. One of them is commemorated by name in the Copthorne Hundred as used in the Domesday Book of 1086. Copped meant it was pollarded. The other was on Ashford Common and is still used in local administration having given its name to the Borough of Spelthorne - the thorn that held you spellbound to keep your word. Its image can be seen in the centre of the borough arms.

Being held sacred has previously protected the trees and so they were often used as boundary markers, especially as they were rooted in the ground and couldn't be moved on dark nights. Several were used to describe the boundary of the lands given to Chertsey Abbey in AD 666.

Hedging was the other main boundary and Hawthorn is ideal for this. Indeed, the word Hawthorn comes from the Saxon word *haga* meaning hedge. Thousands of miles were planted all across the country with the Inclosure Acts of the late 18th and early 19th centuries. An earlier example, for Surrey, is commemorated in the Leatherhead name of Thorncroft, meaning a thorn-hedged enclosure, which was already in existence for inclusion in the Domesday of 1086. Sections of ancient hedge are dotted around the county, where they are often the oldest man-made thing still in use.

35

Under the twiggy hairnet of a low domed head of Hawthorn a trunk and branches have twisted and turned their way through the centuries, defying the appalling growing conditions on the sandstone ridge of Puttenham Common.

Hawthorn gives us the May-blossom of which many people are still so wary they won't have it indoors - the tree is incredibly rich in folklore, both pagan and Christian. The medieval Church had it borne in the processions for Corpus Christi Day (the Thursday following the eighth Sunday after Easter), and they must have used lots of it too, judging by the prices they paid. After the processions the sprays were set up in church before the Lady Altar (the tree symbolised the Immaculate Conception, see Blackthorn). The Church also sanctioned its gathering on either Maundy Thursday or the Eve of the Feast of St. John the Baptist (June 23rd) to use as protection against thunder and lightning, and bringing the wood indoors on Ascension Day ensured a year's good luck.

It was used also to mark burials outside of consecrated ground. These became known as *beggar bushes* from the days when the parish was reluctant to bear the expense of burying any travelling pauper who should unfortunately die within their boundary. Thus ailing travellers were likely to be hastened on their way to the next village. There they were likely to be turned round and sent back. Should they die on the road it was not unknown for the body to be moved over the boundary into the next parish and cause a dispute. The solution was to share the burial expenses between the two parishes and inter the corpse across the boundary so each had half. Then a thorn was planted. A Hawthorn on the Hog's Back, on the boundary between Puttenham and Wanborough, was reputed to be just such a tree. It was grubbed out about 1840 and there among its roots was a human skeleton.

The May Day celebrations were of course pagan but many of the 'traditional' activities are not nearly as old as their promoters would have us believe. The Victorians were surprisingly keen on reviving May Day (despite associating the scent with sex) and so many a 19th century school log book (Ewell's for example) records holidays granted for gathering the May Day blossoms, which were not just those of the thorn. They usually call this *maying* or *garlanding*. An interesting older custom was recalled for me by a lady at Bagshot who remembered she and her sister, as children, being locked in their bedroom on May Day. This was to keep them from the other children whom they could see from the window dancing round a particular thorn tree which they had decorated with strips of coloured rags. I am told this is a tradition from parts of Ireland and leaves me wondering how it came to Bagshot. Could the Irish railway navvies have introduced it?

Looking into the *[illegible]* Pitch Place

Unstead Manor

OAK

Quercus robur L.

Oaks yield famously durable building material as testified by the hundreds and hundreds of timber-framed buildings still surviving, in full working in order, throughout the county.

The oldest surviving houses are thought to date from the 13th century, such as one at Chobham and another at Effingham. Without any documentary evidence these have to be dated on stylistic grounds but occasionally an early document survives to give an exact date. Thus in 1365 the Bishop of Winchester sent two warreners up to Churt to make a new rabbit warren and to build homes for themselves. Those homes still stand and are unique in Surrey for being built in the 'Winchester' style, with king post roofs, rather than the standard Surrey crown post method.

These houses are also impressive memorials to the teams of craftsmen who practised their various skills to such a high standard. Most remain anonymous but there was a Mr. Spong, who died in 1736 at Ockham, and whose epitaph read in part:

Who many a sturdy oak was laid along,
Fell'd by Death's surer hatchet, here lies Spong.
Posts oft he made, yet ne'er a Place could get
And lived by Railing, tho' he was no wit.
Old Saws he had, altho' no Antiquarian;
And Stiles corrected, yet was no great Grammarian...

We can read also of Mr. William Farley of *Kingeston* who, on February 25th 1603, was paid 20 shillings *"for the use of his gynne and gable for the reareing of the timber work of the seconde buildinge"* according to the building accounts for Ashley House at Walton-upon-Thames. It was the town of Kingston-upon-Thames that was one of the great national centres of the building trades. One of the regular customers would have been Sir Eustace de Hacche, a busy royal administrator whose responsibilities included the building works of Edward I's castles. In 1286 he became Lord of Paschenesham Manor next to Leatherhead and was soon engaged upon building work there, for in 1293 he was accused of hi-jacking waggons in Kingston market for taking his timber home!

Another craftsman with royal connections was Mr. Fuller White of Weybridge whose men worked at Hampton Court Palace. They left a message on the underside of a oak floor board which was found during the restoration after the 1986 fire. It reads:
John Trevethan, Joseph Puckeridge, John Gordon, Journeymen to Mr Fuller White, carpenter in Weybridge, relaid this floor, June 1758.

39

Imagine the late 15th century workmen trying to manoeuvre into the nave of Thursley church four massive oak tree trunks, two and half feet thick. Then, with much shouting and panting they winched them upright in exactly the right positions to support the base platform of the new belfry. They did it though. Then the master craftsman braced them all together with beams and arches so securely as to withstand the stresses and strains of bellringing, for all eternity. This he did so, with such a simple but clever design that the view east from the nave to the former great rood was never obstructed.

We were good at that sort of thing in Surrey. It's surprising how many different ways were used to achieve the same result; compare Great Bookham, Bisley, Byfleet, Newdigate and Horley. The most impressive is one next to Horley at Burstow. Here the massive structure is at the west end, created as a separate structure from the main body of the abutting church. You can't imagine the size of the base plinths for the central construction and then that needed massive buttresses to support it, which have to rise from outside that central structure, creating aisles on three sides and the need for lean-to roofs which so attractively mark the tower stages. It's all beautifully textured with a weatherproofing of thousands of oak shingles - something else we were very good at doing. The shingling at Burstow has been reckoned the best in Britain.

Here at the edge of the great Wealden forest there was no doubt a fine tradition of timber crafts. It is probably from Horley or Hurley came one of the greatest master carpenters in Christendom - Thomas Hurley. It was he who created a timber structure like no other, to carry the 400 tons of the central octagon of Ely Cathedral, 94 feet above the floor of the choir. His beams turn Thursley's into tiddlers, for he started the structure with eight supports three feet thick and sixty three feet long! When he died he was succeeded as *King's Chief Carpenter* by that other great medieval genius - Hugh Herland. This is the man who roofed Westminster Hall. They said it couldn't be done because the hall was wider than the length of a tree trunk but Herland came up with an arch braced hammer beam structure that proved them all wrong in all the roof weighs 660 tons and is rated the greatest timber roof in Europe. The oaks came out of the forests by Farnham, while the Herland family, of which there were at least three generations of great master carpenters, are thought to have come from Dunsfold. Hugh ultimately had substantial property at Kingston, among other places. He is probably the only medieval master carpenter of whom a portrait survives - the small figure labelled '*carpentarius*' in the east window of Winchester College Chapel.

Great oak beam constructions still survive in the many barns, notably at Wanborough. The Abinger tithe barn was dismantled and moved to become the banqueting hall at Burford Bridge Hotel, (illus. above).

The finest range of oaken artefacts, of any age, is to be found in our churches and those in Surrey are no exception. Although the county barely gets a mention in most books on the subject, there are, nevertheless, national treasures within their doors. Even the doors themselves at Old Woking and Merstham are of national importance.

Walk up to Dunsfold and you approach a particularly fine building, probably the work of royal masons, which is the only example of its style in the county. Step inside and there the original nave benches survive. With their plain ends, scrolled over at the top and bored with a hole to take a burning taper, they are totally unlike any others in the country and are believed to be coeval with the building and therefore date from c.1270. That makes them the nation's oldest.

For the oldest screen in the country you need to go to Compton. As you walk down the central aisle you will see that the sanctuary of the Norman chancel was vaulted over to support an extra sanctuary above which is open to view from the nave. No other two-storey chancel survives here (but there are three of this type abroad). Being open to the west required the insertion of a safety guard rail, c.1160, which not only makes it the earliest screen but one of the oldest pieces of church woodwork of any sort. By now it's iron hard to the touch but wonderfully tactile as you search for joins and, finding none, realise it was carved out of one massive plank hewn from the heart of an even greater oak. Run your fingers over the sculptured capitals supporting its arches as did the craftsman as he worked it, all those generations ago. If you want to catch sight of a Norman there's a little figure, wearing his chain mail, scratched into the masonry of the chancel arch (low, behind the glass panel).

If you want names for past associates then try Agnes Sander, for it was probably she who sponsored the fine parclose screen in Charlwood church when her husband Richard died in 1480. She had his initials and their coat of arms included

Far, far simpler but even rarer are the wooden fonts at Ash and Chobham (illus.). Only two others occur in England, since they were forbidden by church law. The font had to be decent and a decent font was a stone one. These two may look very plain today but originally they would have been limewashed and then brightly painted with appropriate screens for baptism, one of the Seven Sacraments. That all had to go at the Reformation as indeed did the fonts themselves for a few years. Stone ones were thrown out to become cattle troughs but how these wooden ones survived we'll never know.

in the delicate cresting, animated with angels and winged dragons. This is the county's finest complete screen, very simple and restrained compared with those of East Anglia or the West Country. There's another good one in Gatton church but is of West Country style and therefore probably brought in, like the rest of the furnishings. The local/London school produced the winged, two-legged dragons (wyverns) that uncurl from the corners of the rood screen base at Great Bookham (sketched above), while little dragon heads watch us from the screens at Ewell and Lingfield.

Also at Lingfield is a set of 15th century choir stalls, complete with misericords, from when it was a collegiate church. That was founded in 1431 by Sir Reginald Cobham, eldest son of the Sir Reginald who has the large memorial brass on a tomb nearby. Its heraldry with the three stars appears again in the misericords (dotted sketces). These stalls are of very high quality and far superior to the late Flemish set brought back from the Grand Tour and installed in Gatton church. The whole church has been furnished with Grand Tour trophies, making it the best collection in the county and one of the best in the country.

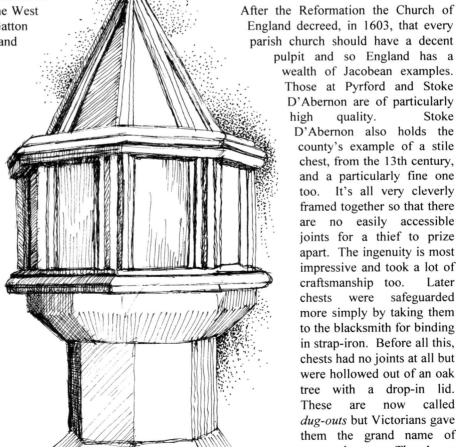

After the Reformation the Church of England decreed, in 1603, that every parish church should have a decent pulpit and so England has a wealth of Jacobean examples. Those at Pyrford and Stoke D'Abernon are of particularly high quality. Stoke D'Abernon also holds the county's example of a stile chest, from the 13th century, and a particularly fine one too. It's all very cleverly framed together so that there are no easily accessible joints for a thief to prize apart. The ingenuity is most impressive and took a lot of craftsmanship too. Later chests were safeguarded more simply by taking them to the blacksmith for binding in strap-iron. Before all this, chests had no joints at all but were hollowed out of an oak tree with a drop-in lid. These are now called *dug-outs* but Victorians gave them the grand name of *monoxylons*. There's a massive one at Betchworth.

Traditionally Oaks were grown as hedgerow trees of which there are some fine lines of mature Oaks around fields at Pyrford. Frequently they were pollarded, of which many hundreds survive, including the Crouch Oak described below. On Ashtead Common is one of the best preserved collections of pollards in Britain and, thankfully, they've been cut again to rejuvenate them for the future. Otherwise they were grown in woods to shelter Hazel coppice beneath. Many acres of this survives but sadly overgrown and neglected, although in some districts, such as at Hambledon, coppicing is being revived. The road from Ewhurst to Forest Green passes through long stretches of this scenery. (The sketch here is from New Haw). Alternatively, the Oaks themselves were coppiced, of which precious little survives in Surrey. Occasionally there's a multi-stemmed Oak to be found to show how they looked but many of these result from an accident in their youth that deprived them of their main stem, rather than having been deliberately coppiced. Oak trees provide a great deal of variety in Surrey, even if there are far too many of them in the wrong places.

What is surprisingly is how few really ancient specimens survive. Two of the best, with easy public access, are at Addlestone and Tilford. The former, known as the Crouch Oak, lives up to its name at the end of Crouch Oak Lane. It's barely more than a timber hulk of a pollarded trunk, about which there are various stories, ranging from it being a boundary Oak for Windsor Great Park, or that the first Queen Elizabeth had a picnic under it, although some would have us believe it was Queen Victoria!

Before Victoria's reign it was known as *Wykliffe's Oak* after John Wycliffe whom, it was said, preached the doctrines of the Reformation beneath it. Wycliffe was the man who inspired the Lollards, and, propounded that the church should not interfere with temporal affairs nor have temporal possessions of its own. He denied the doctrine of transubstantiation and inflamed the Pope even more by supervising the translation of the Bible out of Latin into English

Freshly pollarded oak at Compton 1996

so that 'ordinary' people could read it, for the first time. He died in 1384 at Lutterworth, Leics. where he was rector, but in 1428 the Bishop of Lincoln had his bones exhumed and burnt. Thus in 1828 with the approach of that anniversary there were letters in *The Times*. A monument was proposed for Lutterworth but 'WB' argued for Addlestone: *"I think, therefore, the best monument to the memory of that great man would be, to erect a church upon the scene of his former labours."* Addlestone still did not have its own parish church at that time, being still part of the parish of Chertsey, but in that year of 1828, and presumably not known to 'WB', building work did begin on a church a few yards down the lane from the Oak. Ironically, or appropriately, it was not for the Church of England but for the Nonconformists - the Baptists.

To see this Oak in its more glorious days we need to turn to *Highways and Byways in Surrey,* the first Surrey book by Eric Parker who was then still a young journalist living in Weybridge. He became editor of *The Field* magazine and moved to Hambledon. He went on to write a fine collection of local interest books of which any county could be proud. In his *Surrey Anthology* he wrote: *"When Hugh Thomson in 1907 drew the Crouch Oak at Addlestone for* Highways and Byways in Surrey, *he found a tree in a garden spreading huge branches over a country lane. I went to look at it forty-four years later, in February 1951, and most of the branches had been lopped short. But there it stood, hollow, maimed, but live enough to still drive sap up into its crumpled, crippled limbs. Looking at Hugh Thomson's drawing, I realised he saw branches where we can only guess at them from their stumps. For me, the vision that remains is of a hollow trunk, its bole bulging grey-green bark into February sun and rain..."* (p.206)

In that same year of 1951 Eric Parker also visited that other great Oak, *The King's Oak* on Tilford village green. For the third time in his life he measured it, five feet from the ground, and recorded that the girth had increased to 27 feet 6 inches. Back in 1907 he'd recorded 24 feet 9 inches. Previously, dear old William Cobbett had found it *"full thirty feet round"* some eight or ten feet above the ground! He liked a good story. He told his son, on showing it to him, that when *he* was a little boy it *"was but a very little tree"* but that it had grown into *"by far the finest tree that I ever saw in my life."*

It's always been *The King's Oak*. As *Kynghok* it is said to be mentioned in a charter of 1150 between Henry de Blois, Bishop of Winchester and founder of nearby Farnham Castle, and the monks of Waverley Abbey, also nearby. Hundreds of years later,

another Bishop, Brownlow North, threatened to cut it down and the locals are said to have prevented this by driving metal spikes and nails into the tree. It's still there of course. That's more than can be said for one at Mickleham which on Friday 9th February 1940 was about 60 feet high. That was the day Police Constable Middleton was shaving in the bathroom of the police house in Dell Close and saw through the window that the tree was on the move - perpendicularly. By the time he arrived on the scene, still covered in shaving lather, the tree was standing in the bottom of a huge crater - it's one of those famous Mole Valley 'swallow holes'.

Oaks at Runnymede in 1982; view now blocked by growth of Cherry thickets!
After the Great Storm of 1987 the Queen and Barons planted new Oaks at Runnymede.

ENGLISH ELM

Ulmus procera   Salisb.
and close relatives

Once upon a time, the three gods, Odin, Vili and Ve, were walking the edge of the land where it joins the sea when they came across two fallen trees: an Ash tree and an Elm. They replanted both and then vandalised them - by tearing out the trees' souls. The one from the Ash they endowed with the characteristics of a man and named him Ask. The other was endowed with the characteristics of a woman and she was named Embla. These were the first people, according to this Viking creation myth, and so we are all descended from them. They are our ancestor trees, Ash trees for men, Elm trees for women.

Reverence for this descent can be traced in Surrey by the places founded in their honour. Thus one group of people loyal to Embla is believed to have settled in northern Surrey where its district was ultimately to become the Hundred of Elmbridge, as recorded in the Domesday Book. By then, 1086, it comprised both Moleseys, Apps, Walton-on- Thames, Weston, Weybridge, Esher, Cobham and Stoke D'Abernon (see section on Ash trees for Esher and other Ash-tree place names). Today, that ancient idea has given rise to the modern Borough of Elmbridge.

In the 1970s the great epidemic of Dutch Elm Disease wiped out all the mature Elm trees in Surrey, so that today's young people have no memory of their grandeur. It was not the first time that such an epidemic had swept the country but it will take longer than our lifetimes before Surrey farmland is once again studded with their massive forms billowing green cumulus clouds of leaves. The most famous had been the great avenue (known as 'The Lanes') that stretched for some three- quarters of a mile across Farnham Park up to one of the old castle gateways. Walking the length between the columned trunks with their vaulted branches meeting from either side stirred writers into the usual cathedral images but it was indeed a special walk.

Otherwise they were planted in parks as clumps which were formerly known so aptly as 'plumps'. The great 18th century gardens, such as Claremont, Esher Place and Woburn, all have records of Elm plantings for amenity value. They are of course prone to suddenly shed the odd mature branch ("Elum hateth man and waiteth") and then the timber had over sixty-five uses. It was the great workhorse tree wherever large pieces were needed for rough and ready work.

The notion that it is water resistant has been over simplified. It does resist rotting but only if in permanently saturated conditions. If it is partly in the wet and partly in the dry then it will rot off very quickly at the dividing line. Similarly, it could only be used for timber-framed buildings with care. The beams must not be exposed to the wetting and drying of the weather so in Surrey arose our famous system of hanging tiles over the outside, or sometimes plastering over. During the renovation of what is now the Leatherhead Museum the old rendering was

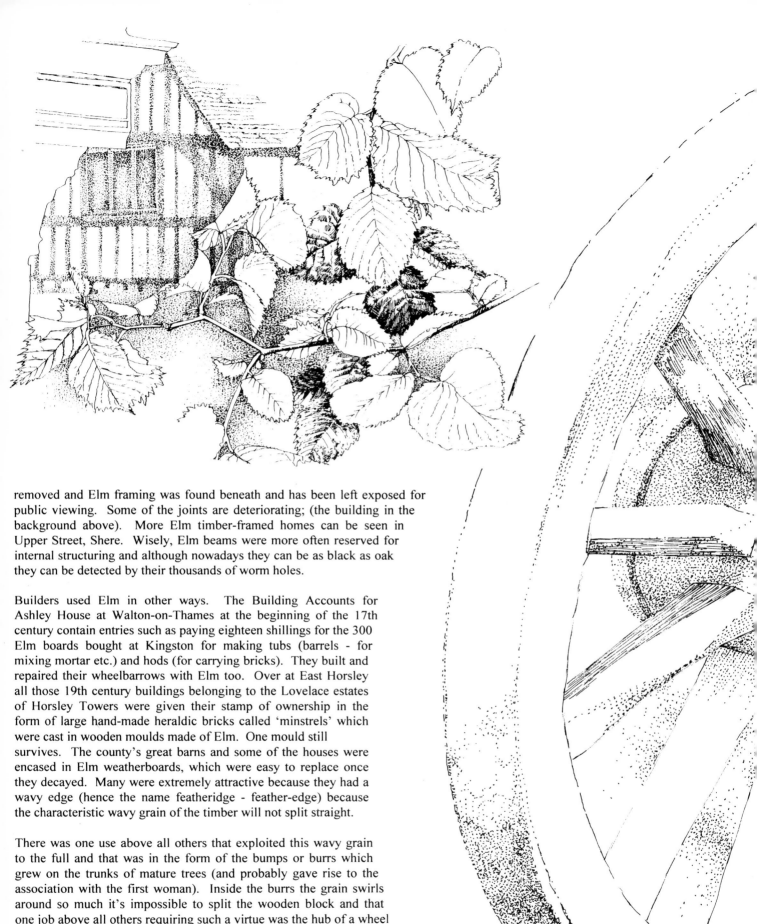

removed and Elm framing was found beneath and has been left exposed for
public viewing. Some of the joints are deteriorating; (the building in the
background above). More Elm timber-framed homes can be seen in
Upper Street, Shere. Wisely, Elm beams were more often reserved for
internal structuring and although nowadays they can be as black as oak
they can be detected by their thousands of worm holes.

Builders used Elm in other ways. The Building Accounts for
Ashley House at Walton-on-Thames at the beginning of the 17th
century contain entries such as paying eighteen shillings for the 300
Elm boards bought at Kingston for making tubs (barrels - for
mixing mortar etc.) and hods (for carrying bricks). They built and
repaired their wheelbarrows with Elm too. Over at East Horsley
all those 19th century buildings belonging to the Lovelace estates
of Horsley Towers were given their stamp of ownership in the
form of large hand-made heraldic bricks called 'minstrels' which
were cast in wooden moulds made of Elm. One mould still
survives. The county's great barns and some of the houses were
encased in Elm weatherboards, which were easy to replace once
they decayed. Many were extremely attractive because they had a
wavy edge (hence the name featheridge - feather-edge) because
the characteristic wavy grain of the timber will not split straight.

There was one use above all others that exploited this wavy grain
to the full and that was in the form of the bumps or burrs which
grew on the trunks of mature trees (and probably gave rise to the
association with the first woman). Inside the burrs the grain swirls
around so much it's impossible to split the wooden block and that
one job above all others requiring such a virtue was the hub of a wheel
- so that the spokes could be driven in all round without risk of splitting
the block. Thus we men have to concede that it's the ladies who have
kept the world's wheels turning!

RIGHT : Restoring spokes into the nave, hub or stock of a wheel. Although wheelrights were
once commonplace in Surrey the illustrations in this book required travelling far beyond Surrey,
especially to record women working alongside the men in the old family tradition.

WEEPING WILLOW

Salix babylonica L.
Salix x sepulchralis Simonkai

Hump-backed, bent double, trailing skirts of golden twigs in the waterside, like old washer-women at work, the Weeping Willows are a much-loved feature beside our lakes and rivers. They are not British but, like the Cedar of Lebanon, they've won such a place in the hearts of so many that our landscapes wouldn't be quite the same without them.

Despite storm after storm those incredible long pendulous twigs never seem to get entangled. That's more than can be said for their history! To start with, there are two different trees which we recognise as a Weeping Willow, although one is now extremely rare. That is sometimes called the Chinese Weeping Willow because it did indeed come from China, yet its specific name is *babylonica*. It wasn't known in Babylon until it was introduced there, but Linnaeus chose that name because of lines in Psalm 137:

> *By the rivers of*
> *Babylon,*
> *There we sat down, yea*
> *we wept,*
> *When we remembered*
> *Zion.*
> *We hanged our harps*
> *Upon the willows of*
> *the midst thereof.*
> *(King James's Bible)*

Possibly they didn't hang there harps on a willow at all. Some people think it was most likely a Poplar, *Populus euphratica*. The British stock did come from the Euphrates, about 1730, although it may have been tried earlier, with a planting at Kew in 1692. It's not entirely hardy so early attempts might have been thwarted. However, in the 1730s it was planted in Twickenham Park, supposedly by a Mr. Vernon, or, in unnamed stories, by "a merchant from Aleppo".

Another story of its introduction has the poet Alexander Pope planting it at Twickenham from a cutting he'd rooted from a twig used as parcel binding by a friend of his in Spain. Don't go and look for it. Pope's successor had it cut down because he resented the loss of privacy occasioned by the tourists it attracted.

Nearly all of today's trees are known as the Common or Golden Weeping Willow, *Salix x sepulchralis*, which is a hybrid between *S. babylonica* and the White Willow, *S. alba* but you'll find a lot of names have been used in this tangle. The hybrid is thought to have come from France about 1800 but even that's not certain. Records do show that some form of Weeping Willows were planted in Surrey's great gardens, such as Woburn Farm (Chertsey) and Portmore Park (Weybridge) in the 18th century. The latter had them planted by the water cascades where they must have created a fine scene.

Another source of our trees has been the island of St. Helena, where Napoleon had one sent out from Britain in 1810. It succumbed to a storm but cuttings were taken and planted around his grave. They didn't root but another lot taken in 1828 did and it's from these that some in Britain are claimed to descend. There's one in Gatton Park for example. A more famous one was at Elmbank, Lower Halliford. This was the final home of the writer Thomas Love Peacock, and he had one sent him from St. Helena by Sir Hudson Lowe, who was Governor during Napoleon's exile.

Perhaps the most amazing one of all is *inside* the parish church at Great Bookham. It's a memorial, of about 1830, to Elizabeth Andrews and relatives and thus the tree is of stone, growing up the north chancel wall and sweeping round a window in an altogether startling way. It tries to be so realistic there's even an iron railing round the trunk to protect it from the choir boys!

Illus. - Ruins of St. Catherine's Chapel through the Weeping Willows by the Godalming Navigation at Guildford.

TULIP TREE

Liriodendron tulipifera L.

Among the early stories to return to this country from the new colony of Virginia was of the way some of the native peoples (the Cherokee) travelled by canoe. These they hollowed out from the trunks of great trees which they called *Rakiok* but we call it the Tulip Tree from the likeness of the flowers. The earliest reference is from 1590 in Thomas Harriot's *A Briefe and True Report of the New Found Land of Virginia* wherein he says *"the inhabitants that were neere unto us doe commonly make their boats or Canoes of the form of trowes [troughs] only with the helpe of fire, hartchets of stones, and shels; we have known some of so great being made in that sort of one tree that they have carried well xx men at once, besides much baggage..."* In 1612 Captain John Smith, in his *Description of Virginia and Proceedings of the Colony* refers again to the techniques of using fire and stones to make the canoes: *"Some of them are an elne [ell] deep, and 40 or 50 foot in length, and some will beare 40 men, but the most ordinary are smaller, and will beare 10, 20, or 30, according to their bignes [bigness]."* The early writers also noted the difficulty with which these boats were steered and marvelled at the skills involved in success. What thoughts to stir the imagination, standing out on the lawn on an English summer's afternoon, looking up through the spreading boughs of a mature Tulip Tree!

It wasn't long before the tree had been introduced here. It was listed by Henry Wise in 1663. The Bishop of London had one planted at Fulham Palace by 1688. By then the bulbous Tulip was well established but the periods of 'Tulipmania' in Europe were still within memory so the news of a *tree* that bore Tulip flowers must have been a source of wonder indeed. It required patience too, for not only did John Evelyn observe that the seed was slow to germinate, but the tree won't flower till it matures and even then it needs a long hot American-style summer to bring out its best. The first time one flowered in England was at Portmore Park in Weybridge, (where new Tulip Trees have been planted beside the A317).

After much waiting, those famous tulip-shaped blooms can prove very disappointing; yet their admirers wax lyrical - even the academic entries in the Royal Horticultural Society's *Dictionary* yield to emotion on this count - *"The delicately scented pale green flowers are usually visible only at close quarters but they are beautiful when cut and displayed where the elegant vase-shaped form and internal markings can be appreciated."* They are among the largest single blooms of any tree in Britain, but outrivalled by their close relatives, the Magnolias.

Timber was the original eye-catcher, remember, and, with trees rising nearly 200 feet with trunks 10 feet in diameter, in favoured states like Ohio and Florida, there was plenty of that timber. In commercial circles it was traded as Tulip Poplar, Yellow Poplar or White Poplar, but it is best known as America's famous Whitewood. It is not a true Poplar but in early America, before Linnaeus classified the plant world more accurately, it was called Poplar after the similarity of its white wood. William Cobbett could see commercial value in that and promoted the Tulip Tree as he did the Robinia.

At Esher Place is one reputed to be the largest and oldest in the country and another of the nation's finest stands in the lawn of Field Place at Compton, while new ones have been planted by the National Trust in the lawn on the south side of Hatchlands. Even without their flowers they have a noble habit of growth and their soft green leaves turn rich butter yellow in autumn. These are almost unique for being square ended as though the points have been cut off with scissors.

49

ASH

Fraxinus excelsior L.

The beautiful Ash tree, so common in Surrey, was dubbed *The Lady of the Woods* and *Venus of the Woods* in later times. Ironically, in early times, this tree was considered by some cultures to be the ancestor of all *men*. The Viking gods Odin, Vili and Ve drew the soul out of a fallen Ash and endowed it with the charateristics of a man which was wedded to the soul of an Elm tree endowed as a woman and from this union all the people on earth were believed to have descended. Ancestor worship was important to the early cultures and so we should expect there to have been sacred groves of these trees in Surrey. Two places are known to be named after the *aesc* or Ash trees, namely Eashing and Esher, while in Spelthorne there was Echelford, modernised as Ashford, although the older spelling is still used for Echelford School etc. Sacred groves do not usually leave archaeological evidence so in Surrey we are very ignorant of the locations of such sites but these place-names may well be providing linguistic evidence. Tree worship was still being practised long after the coming of Christianity [Chertsey Abbey founded 666] and was still so rife in the 11th century that King Cnut had to outlaw it by the law of the land.

Ash timber is Britain's best where high tensile strength and shock absorbancy are required, making it ideal for such uses as wheel spokes and tool handles. The characteristics of our timbers have been known for thousands of years and striking proof came locally from the Bronze Age when a hand axe was excavated a few years ago in the gravel workings between Chertsey and Shepperton It was heralded as the first to survive complete with its woodwork and was thus of great international importance, especially as it proved to be of a different construction than ever imagined before. Successful fund-raising ensured it was conserved and retained in Surrey and it fell to me to drive round to East London and bring this axe back to Chertsey Museum from the conservation laboratories. That gave me the chance to ask the experts if they had analysed the trees employed. Sure enough, the handle was of Ash; (the headpiece was of Oak). Today a good axe still has an Ash handle but sadly our tool would be inferior to the Bronze Age one, for their design with the headpiece, gave the axe twice the mechanical efficiency of today's. In other words, in comparison, they could fell a tree twice as quickly as we could or take the same time but only use half the energy. This pronouncement from the physicists was tested by archaeologists, using a replica, and was found to be true. Today, we think we are so clever!

(Illus. approx. life-size)

50

At the other end of the time scale there are many people who remember that during the 1950s and 1960s the Ash tree was prominent in schoolchild lore, in places such as Albury and Haslemere. Come Ash Wednesday it was crucial to arrive at school with an Ash twig, which was normally kept concealed. Upon being challenged to produce it, by another child, it was equally crucial to defeat their doubt by suddenly brandishing the twig. That saved the child from having their feet stamped upon by the challenger and very often all other nearby children. Girls were sometimes given the alternative punishment of being pushed into the stinging nettles if there were any adjacent. This was not such a problem at Haslemere because the C. of E. Primary School in Chestnut Avenue took the classes to the parish church for a service on each Wednesday morning in Lent and the route of the crocodile through Pathfields had its clumps of wayside nettles. Teachers were allowed to box ears in those days and so at the Ash Wednesday service there was much snivelling. Cheats suffered most. Woe betide a child who presented a twig from anything other than an Ash and of course only the Ash has black buds so the impromptu juries had little trouble reaching their decision. Less certain is the origin of this ritual (which, in common with other childhood rituals, had to end at noon) but it would seem to be a transference of the oak leaf/oak apple ritual from Royal Oak Day on May 29th, to celebrate the Restoration of the monarchy with King Charles II in 1660

Haslemere Parish Church

It was coppiced Ash that yielded the long straight poles needed for supporting Hops being grown for brewing. It was on the clays of West Surrey around Farnham, and over the Hampshire border down through Alton where the main hop-growing areas became settled. The Ash grew well on the adjoining areas and was an important crop. The *stools* (or *stoles* to some people) had their shoots thinned to about five and these were left to grow on for 12-25 years until they could yield a good 15 feet of pole. Then they were cut, in the winter, ready for insertion in the *hills* next spring. Hills were the mounds into which the Hops were planted and each took three poles. The hills stretched in rows across the *grounds* as they were called in Surrey, (*gardens* in Kent), anything, so long as they were not *fields*, because fields were at one time taxed and the brewers were not going to fall for that one!

The last Surrey hop grounds - at Puttenham. Sketched 1990. The system of strings between the poles do not show up on this scale.

Bringing home the hop poles from the woods was an annual event but could still be memorable. George Sturt, the Farnham wheelwright, recorded the following from Fred Bettesworth, an old Surrey labourer:- *"He was miles from home. The tracks through the coppice - you could not call them roads - were knee-deep in mud. There were two horses for the solitary young man to manage, and of course a two-horse load of poles to be got home on the long pole-carriage. Wherefore it happened that the heavily loaded 'carriage' stuck fast in deep clay, upon which it behoved Bettesworth to unload, get horses and pole-carriage out of the hole they had sunk in, and then replace the load. Once, or twice even, this might have been borne, but six times it happened - six times he had to unload and re-load those icy poles, snow and rain swirling through the coppice all the time, mud begriming him, his beloved horses suffering, his own hands chapped and raw from handling the half-frozen poles. Long after dark he got home tired out; but there were the horses to see to...."* (George Bourne *The Bettesworth Book*, 1901, p.30)

In 1659 Samuel Hartlibb reported "Now it is known that Hoppes of England are best in the world." Ten years later John Worlidge reported that two acres of Hampshire hops returned as much profit as 50 acres of arable land.

It's hardly surprising then, that in 1724 Daniel Defoe commented on "the most surprising increase in hop grounds." By 1878 there were 72, 000 acres around Alton/Farnham. They needed hundreds of thousands of poles. These were not only of Ash but also Sweet Chestnut and conifer thinnings such as Larch.

In the 1950s hopping was modernised and improved plant breeding produced new strains with a much higher acid content. This reduced the need for so many acres. The rise in lager drinking reduced the need further as most brews had to be made from a continental recipe, not from English hops.

BEECH
Fagus sylvatica L.

The Beech was one of the great workhorse trees of the Romans so we can imagine the dismay of Julius Caesar when he reported that there were no Beech trees in Britain. He didn't look in the right places but they were undoubtedly a great rarity compared with today. That made Beeches sufficiently special to be commemorated in place-names, but significantly, in Surrey, there's only one of importance - Bookham. Both *book* and *Beech* derive from the same Old English, from when Beech tablets were used for writing upon, whether in Norse runes or the Arabic script. The smooth white inner surface of the scrolled bark from a young bough was also exploited. One of the reasons for King Alfred the Great's greatness was the way he wrote down military directives to send to his leaders, whom he'd taught to read. If intercepted by his Viking opponents he knew they couldn't read the script and neither could he be betrayed by an illiterate messenger. Soon *book* was a verb, meaning to be assigned by written charter, which implies some place-names may record foundation by charter rather than being connected directly with Beech trees.

Certainly there never used to be great beechwoods over the Downs to which we have become accustomed in more recent times, such as those clothing the hillsides around Caterham and Woldingham. This throws doubt on statements that Surrey's medieval glass industry was fuelled with Beech faggots. The tree was only just getting a hold then, following the clearance of more oakwoods from the chalk downs in the 13th century. Even four hundred years later the increase in beechwoods was causing John Evelyn to ponder the reason. He expected Oak seedlings to regenerate where the old Oaks had been felled, rather than Beech. They probably did but Beech will germinate much better in shade and very soon the beechlings cast their own shade to the discomfort of the oaklings which grow more slowly. Even in the early 19th century this process was still in action and causing William Cobbett to ponder the success of the Beech.

By the time the land owners were improving their parks the tree was high in popularity for its beauty, for that unique sleek character that catches eye and heart. What a grand scene was invoked by Martin Tupper when he described the *"placid loveliness"* of the Silent Pool at Albury with *"great silver beeches stretching as to shake hands across the clear deep water, edged with greenery all round, but in a pure white shelving basin of chalk."*

That was Victorian but it was the Georgians before them who had planted the saplings with an eye to that beauty in the future. The great 18th century landscape gardens, such as Claremont, Esher Place, Painshill, and Woburn, all had Beeches planted. Where there was plenty of room they were also planted as avenues, of which the best known was planted from Bookham up the Downs to Polesden Lacey. This suffered badly in the Great Storm of 1987 but the National Trust has replanted.

Another grand avenue took visitors for a quarter of a mile over the heath to Chobham Place. In recent times that became submerged in surrounding woodlands until Surrey Heath Borough Council set about restoration. After three years the first phase was 're-opened' to the public in 1997 and now visitors to Chobham Woods can once again follow the carriageway between stately trees and watch the sapling replacements filling the gaps year by year. At the end nearest the house four massive old Beeches survive which are thought to remain from the original plantings made by the Thomas brothers, Anthony and Gainsford, who owned the estate successively from 1697-1721.

Single trees have been employed regularly for commemorative plantings. At Addlestone the head teacher wrote in St.Augustine's school log book, on November 3rd 1937, *"One child chosen to plant a Beech tree in Victory Park in commemmoration of the coronation of H. M. George VI. Monica Yates to be taken to Victory Park on November 20th for the ceremony at 3pm."*

More Beech is used in our homes today than any other native hardwood, not to mention the thousands of desks and chairs in schools and offices. That would have astounded John Evelyn who loathed the timber - *"I wish the use of it were, by a law, prohibited all joiners, cabinet-makers, and such as furnish tables, chairs, bedsteads, coffers, screws, etc. They have a way to black and polish it, so as to render it like Ebony, and with a mixture of soot and urine, imitate the Walnut; but as the colour does not last, so neither does the wood itself (for I can hardly call it timber) soon after the worm has seized it, unless one sponge and imbibe it with the Oil of Spike, where they have made holes."*
(Silva; 47; spelling modernised)

Despite this, Beech is as strong or stronger than Oak in some tests. That depends of course upon knowing just when to fell or throw the trees and at what time intervals thereafter to begin opening the trunks and working the timber. Beech requires a lot of skill, as recalled by Farnham's famous wheelwright, George Sturt, just after the First World War;- *"During the war vast quantities of beech were spoiled in the prevailing ignorance when to throw it and open the timber. Spoiled, I mean, for old-fashioned wheelwright work, chiefly in axle-trees. For this purpose beech should be as hard as bone, and therefore should be cut down in November (they used to say in my shop) and opened into quarters by Christmas."* The wheelrights also ranked it with Elm and Ash for forming the sections or *felloes* (pronounced fellies in Britain) that make the rim of a wheel. Under compression Beech is very strong so when the hot iron tyre cools and shrinks round the new wheel it withstands the compression. The contraction forces the spokes tight into their mortices in both felloe and hub until all is locked powerfully together. So powerful is the tension that the wheel has to be clamped down during the cooling of the tyre for fear it will explode up in the wheelwrights' faces.

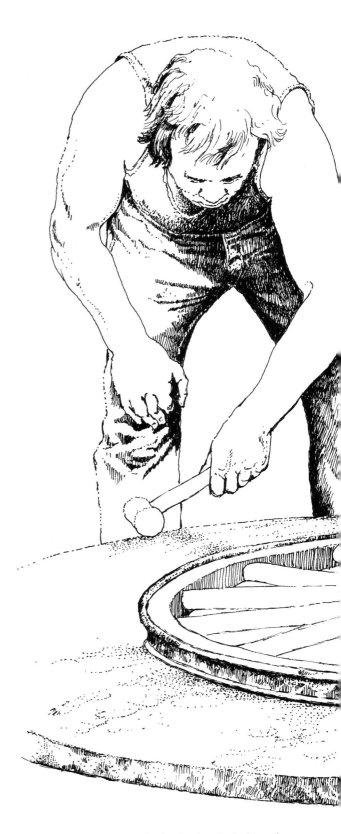

ABOVE - The metal tyre, after heating in a fire is dropped over the wooden wheel which bursts into flames but is instantly drenched. The cooling metal contracts around the woodwork and the wheelwright gives the final blows to marry them together. Note the central clamp that holds the wheel down onto the base plate and prevents it exploding upwards under the force of the compression.

ABOVE - Using a spoke-shave, the wheelwright chamfers off the edges of the felloes between the spokes. This is to reduce weight, for the benefit of the horses, and the art lies in knowing how much to shave off and where, without reducing the strength of the construction.

ROBINIA

Robinia pseudoacacia L.

The beautiful Robinia is one of the trees that could claim importance in Surrey, for it was promoted heavily by William Cobbett of *Rural Rides* fame. He was born in Farnham in 1762 at the *Jolly Farmer* pub (now the *William Cobbett*) which is the timber framed gable ahead of those crossing Long Bridge out of lower Farnham. He's one of those who rose to fame from humble beginnings. To many he was infamous! He was very good with words, whether with his pen or his mouth, becoming an anti-establishment radical campaigner from 1805. He wouldn't budge from his views, even to the extent of going to prison (1810-12) for opposing the flogging of militiamen, and he knew full well that a prison sentence in his days was so often a death sentence from 'jail fever' and other diseases. He wasn't out long before he was leading the post-1815 reform movement but by 1817 he deemed it wise to go off to America for a couple of years. There he became enthused with the Robinia.

It's a native of Eastern North America from the Appalachians and Pennsylvania to Northern Georgia and there it was called the Locust. Apparently early missionaries had used this tree to illustrate John the Baptist's diet of 'locusts and honey' while in the wilderness, for the natives boiled the oily seeds to make a much-esteemed meal (don't try it - the seeds contain poisons!). They also used the wood. It's very tough and difficult to work but is extremely durable, and hardens with age rather than rotting, so in America it was used later for railway sleepers. In Cobbett's day, its uses included pulleys and owels, reflected in one of its American names - *Treenail*. Just what we need back home, thought Cobbett, for the shipwrights, who need thousands of wooden pins for their constructions. They can't get enough Oak beams and planks either but the Locust could be used for both ship and house building.

The William Cobbett from Long Bridge 1990

Back he came with his ideas. The tree was already available from our nurseries, as Robinia, but was not proving very saleable. Cobbett therefore bought up the stocks and launched into one of his impassioned campaigns to resell them, under the unfamiliar American name of Locust-tree. His sales patter was well up to standard and the gullible were soon investing in what they were led to believe was a new American wonder tree. He made quite outrageous claims for the timber and on the back of these promises he sold over a million trees and made vast profits. That's more than can be said for the landowners who bought the saplings. They did not see their investment mature into highly desirable timber trees for shipbuilding, since ships were now being built of iron!

Cobbett eventually retired to be a country farmer, albeit a pioneering one, at Normandy just outside his birthplace at Farnham. He died in 1835 and was buried in Farnham churchyard - the table-tomb by the north door. Some of Cobbett's original trees are preserved along Queen Elizabeth's Walk at Barnes where he had a farm.

His Robinia trees live on and have naturalised into all but two small districts of Surrey. There are fine mature ones in many gardens but some strains are particularly prone to sucker from the rootstocks which is not a popular habit in lawns! In the countryside it leads to some grand thickets which in years like 1997 flower particularly profusely, filling the air with fragrance from their short tassels of white pea-like blooms. They are used in the perfume industry.

Once again it's high in the popularity ratings since golden-leaved cultivars have become available. These are being used as amenity trees in public places just as were the green ones. They are surface-rooting which is not always an advantage on some sites, but on the other hand, they do not have widely spreading branches. Their branching pattern is very distinctive in winter and then the wonderful trunks show their deep fissures, unlike anything else in Britain.

Evelyn urged their use for avenues but in Surrey that has never been taken up on an impressive scale. There are a few alongside the eastern half of Wych Hill Lane in Woking but these are now over-mature and due for felling. Happily, the Borough Council is aware of their importance and has already ordered their replacements. Indeed they've ordered sixty four! These will be interplanted between the existing trees in readiness for when the mature ones have to go. No doubt that would have pleased the Frenchman Jean Robin, after whom the tree was named by Linnaeus in the 18th century. Jean Robin (1550-1629) served three Kings as their royal gardener, nurseryman and herbalist at the Louvre and at what became the Jardin des Plantes. He introduced many American plants into European cultivation and was succeeded by his son who was the first to grow the tree in Europe, in 1635.

Cobbett's. Normandy 94.

BIRCH

Silver Birch
Betula pendula Roth

Downy Birch
Betula pubescens Ehrh

Haslemere
Manor.

Haslemere Manor House is one of only five good houses in Surrey of Carolean architecture but this site on its dry sandy hillside above the wet claylands of Holdfast knew earlier houses. The manor house was known in 1219 as Bercherst, meaning Birch clearing. Travel northwards (A286) and nameboards herald Lower Birtley which in the time of Edward I was a farm in his royal manor of Witley; Upper Birtley is on the right at the top of the next rise. Their name comes from Byrkley meaning a Birch tree clearing or wood. Another Birch clearing (Berkele in 1231) gave rise to Birtley House, not very far away in Bramley. Byrkley-type names gave rise to the modern name Barclay so that Blackmore Heath at Horsley was formerly Barclay, derived from one Thomas de Berkle.

These are not only local testaments to the presence and importance of Birch in the early Middle Ages but are national scarcities in the South Country. Not often does the Birch tree occur in names and charters because it is a gregarious tree and of mixed woodlands at that, rarely serving as a useful landmark tree, but in parts of Surrey the very woodlands were made of Birch. Today this invasive habit on the sandy soils gets it dubbed 'The Surrey Weed.'

Surrey people have always found a multitude of uses for the Birch. For something of particular note we need to think of horse racing, for at Albury are the workshops of *Gill and Punter*, Britain's foremost manufacturers of fences. They work with natural materials, primarily Birch and Ash but sometimes Oak and Furze (although Furze is to be banned on British racecourses from 2000), rather than plastic. Oh yes, someone's invented plastic twigs for the fences!

The Birch is cut throughout the year. That's a full-time job for at least four cutters since so much is needed - there are over fifty racecourses in Britain. Surrey cannot provide enough, until someone starts cropping it specifically, so there's a constant search for more from outside the county. It's cut with a billhook so that the downward blow leaves a point on the stem and it is this nicety that raises *Gill and Punter* above their competitors, for a point is much needed when it comes to forcing the ends into the ground. Other people harvest with a chain-saw which leaves blunt squared-off ends.

Once cut, the stems are bound into small workable bundles of about six main stems (a bit thinner at the butt end than a broom handle and reaching well over head height) and a handful of lesser cuttings. They are either 'brown' or 'green' depending whether they have leaves on or not. All Class I racecourses, such as Cheltenham and Doncaster, demand the brown which means the other courses have to accept green or part green, because there just isn't enough brown birch to go round. Even if a year's demand could be cut in a winter there would be the problem at the end of the season that last winter's twigs had become brittle.

Back at the yard the base structure has been constructed of softwood (sometimes Oak for a permanent fence) to which are added double 'fence' sections constructed of legs and cross rails like a gate. Between these double fences the tallest, stoutest Birch is packed very tightly (courtesy of the pressure exerted by a fork-lift truck!). The lesser stems are woven vertically through the rails of the structure and more are built in horizontally to widen out the base. When it's all built it is trimmed down to the statutory height and is ready for transporting. When in place they will stretch 35-40 feet across the course.

Places like Cork always want these ready-to-use versions whereas some others buy only the structure and the Birch ready for their own workforces to make up. Birch is also ordered in bundles, by the thousand, for repairing existing fences. Cheltenham needs about 3,000 brown bundles a year plus green bundles for repairs.

RIGHT - sketches from the fencing yard of 'Gill and Punter', 1998.

Lower left - the size of the Birch bundles, with 'brown' (leafless) on the left and 'green' (leafy) on the right.

Top Right - Breaking the Birch bundle and sorting the stems to begin weaving the central upright section of the fence. The framework of the fence is Ash wood, for its natural combination of strength with flexibility, to with- stand the impact of a racehorse.

Bottom Right - Weaving the central section of the lowest size of fence. There are three sizes. The tallest meets the exact specifications for the races but there are two lower sizes which are used for training.

Mr. Bob Underdown
Master fence-maker, 'Gill and Punter', 1998

HORSE CHESTNUT
Aesculus hippocastanum L.

*The massive Horse Chestnut in
Haslemere High Street, 1998,
beside the former Georgian Hotel.*

There are only a few significant landmark trees in Surrey and among these must be the Horse Chestnut, or 'conker tree' in Haslemere High Street. Although not recorded until the beginning of the twentieth century, tradition has the sexton planting it in 1792. It's size indicates such a date, making it one of the oldest, if not *the* oldest in Surrey. It stands beside the street's grandest building, dating from the 16th century but extensively rebuilt in the 18th century (Grade II Listed) in Queen Anne style. The front porch was added in the 1930s by local architect Allen Chandler, using a design from a book on American Colonial architecture, for in 1928 the building was modernised in honour of General James Oglethorpe (1696-1785), founder of the American state of Georgia. He was also the local MP and associated with this site. Thus for much of the 20th century this was the Georgian Hotel, with Oglethorpe pictured on the sign, until October 6th 1997 when the hotel was closed down suddenly and unexpectedly. For other old Horse Chestnut trees in Surrey visit Nonsuch Park but the one outside Thursley church, that has been used to illustrate books about trees, stands no more.

Horse Chestnuts may look very much at home here and be much loved by the British but are not in fact native. They come from Albania and Greece and were introduced at the very beginning of the 1600s. Then in 1711 came the New World version, with red flowers, the American Red Buckeye, *Aesculus pavia.* Then the two hybridized (in Germany) in the early 19th century to give the familiar Red Horse Chestnut, *Aesculus x carnea.* These, with the white, make a grand floral display around the park in Chobham where they were planted as a memorial to those villagers who died in the Second World War. Older, was the avenue planted in 1908 in Woking Park. Only part of this survived the Great Storm of 1987. Older still, is the long avenue planted in about 1895 to mark the boundary between Sunbury and Kempton. It stretches along the roadside for nearly a mile.

They are not just amenity trees but have a variety of uses. The conkers are rich in glycerine so in the First World War, Queen Mary included the gathering of conkers in her salvage schemes. The glycerine was much needed for munitions, for the highly explosive nitroglycerine. Another scheme had people gathering them for animal feed, as the children did in Hersham in 1916. A ton of conkers saved using half a ton of corn. Such feeding, and other culinary uses for people, should not be embarked upon today without due regard to the extraction of the toxic compounds. You may already be using conkers in your shampoo!

The prime importance has always been using the conkers as medicine for *"broken winded"* horses (and cattle), hence *Horse* Chestnut. There are at least four other explanations for the name but the oldest is the horse medicine one. It's used in the tree's Greek homeland and in Turkey and so was the explanation given by Evelyn. From those countries the knowledge was shared with those great horsemen, the Arabs, who still use it. Perhaps bearing this out is the frequency with which Horse Chestnuts have been planted beside the village smithy, in the days when the smith was the local farrier as well. The white blooms show up well in black-and-white photos and so many an early photographer chose blossom time to record the smithy *"underneath the spreading Chestnut tree."* In other words, the farriers grew their own medicine.

Elsewhere there are more natural plantings and many self-seeded trees. They merge in with the British greenery surprisingly well, as along the edge of the wood behind Outwood green. The white blossom blends naturally with the English spring succession, through the whites of Blackthorn, Cherry, Pear and Hawthorn - *"it bears a most glorious flower"* noted John Evelyn. who expressed a wish that we should plant more of them - they were still quite new in his day. He wasn't very responsive to autumn colour but the Horse Chestnut is often the starter of that season, with soft yellow, flushed so often with orange and salmon, before turning gold and finally rusting away on the wet ground.

This is the foremost tree of childhood in Britain. In spring the *sticky buds* were handfulled off to junior school for jarring on teacher's desk and later the autumn term opened with the playground conker championship. George Sturt remembered harvesting them in Farnham Park in the 1860s:

> *"To throw among the horse chestnuts stick or stone so as to bring down the glossy nuts was an adventure of breathless interest, though I myself was hardly brave enough for it."*

Walnuts grow fine upright boughs when close-grown, like Oak trees, but, given space they spread into a grand dome, just like Oak trees.

WALNUT
Juglans regia L.

At any time of the year the Walnut is a beautiful tree but in summer there is the added virtue of the aromatic foliage - a glorious summer smell to some of us but alas not appreciated by all! It's the same with the chunky crimson catkins, which only those few with sharp eyes notice bursting out amid tiny leaves from the buds at the end of May. Everything else is burgeoning at this time and so these tend to get overlooked nowadays. Not so in the past. They foretold a great and valuable harvest, so long as a late frost didn't get them, and to this end they were watched over anxiously.

The Walnut was one of our most valuable trees, in the south, where the catkins were most likely to escape a late frosting and so develop into nuts. Today we no longer use walnuts as a major food source but turn our thoughts to the timber, yet the word Walnut to describe timber dates only from 1585, according to the Oxford English Dictionary. A broader view of the tree, at different times of the year, reveals at least 79 different uses and that's if all joiners' and cabinet makers' work are lumped together as 'furniture'.

When Aubrey recorded Banstead he noted the Walnuts: "This place affords a great Quantity of Wallnuts, (a Fruit the County it self abounds much in) perhaps more than all England besides)." He added that "the Effluvia of the leaves sweeten and correct the air" but in fact they were avoided as a strewing herb because they induce headaches in some people - hence one of the Greek names for Walnut was 'Karuon' meaning headache.

TABLE MANNERS - Walnuts finished off the meals in the great houses, whether monastic or secular, and in the Benedictine Houses, like Chertsey Abbey, the Rule decreed the monks must open their nuts with their knife and not their teeth!
Image from the 14thC. glass in Worplesdon church.

The tree is not native but authorities debate whether it was introduced by the Romans or in the later Middle Ages. The latter cannot be true for Walnuts are present in estate records throughout the medieval period. A Roman introduction, therefore, seems most likely, especially as the Romans held Walnuts sacred, dedicated to Jove, and considered the fruit a great delicacy. Importation must have been slow and expensive so surely the Romans, who were keen gardeners, tried growing their own - if any nuts were left in a damp cold outhouse they would have sprouted readily in the spring. As for the later Middle Ages, that was when hardier strains were introduced and these have confused the issue.

The name testifies to an early date too since Walnut occurs in various forms (*walh-hnutu, walnuss, walnote, walhnot*) in the early languages of N. W. Europe, to be brought here by those peoples, such as the Saxons. Their word led to *Walshnutte*, where *walsh* meant *foreign*. In other words, this tree, from S. E. Europe and the Middle East through to Afghanistan, was foreign to them when they encountered it. Of course, to the Saxons, the native Romano-British were foreign too. These walsh people were driven west into *Wal*es (Welsh), and down into Cornwall - hence the *wall* on the county name. Those that wouldn't budge gathered into their own *walsh* communities, such as *Wal*ton-on-Thames and *Wal*ton-on-the-Hill in Surrey.

These racial distinctions may well have given rise to our prejudices against red hair; prejudices between the black-haired Saxons and the red-haired Celts. Woe betide a Saxon girl who gave birth to a red-haired child - somebody had been over Offa's Dyke !! Thus it was said anyone born with red hair had been fathered by the Devil - even our Royal House of Plantagenet was derided as 'the Devil's brood'. Consequently red hair dye has rarely been in demand but should there be a call for it then those beautiful Walnut catkins and the freshly formed nuts will do the job. Both Saxon and Roman ladies considered black hair very desirable and to that end dye was made from the hard nut shells, and continued so throughout the Middle Ages. By the 17th century the fashion had changed to yellow, yes yellow, and the dye could be obtained from green shells, while the leaves yielded a suitable brown, right up to the 20th century.

The most significant uses of the tree centred upon food and oil from the nuts. Surviving medieval accounts show that special Walnut orchards were planted and the surplus sold off, whether by the Church, as was the case with the monastery at Norwich, or by the great landowners, such as the Earl of Cornwall, who held Byfleet manor in Surrey. It was the county reputed to have the most and also the best, although the latter claim may just be good marketing!

Mass plantings began again in the 17th century, with much promotion from John Evelyn, and towards the end of the 18th century these were significant enough for demarcation on the maps - "upwards of 10,000 Walnut trees do grow hereabouts" wrote one surveyor over the map at Walton-on-the-Hill, while Sir Richard Stidolph advertised 40,000 Walnut trees on his Norbury Park estates when he put them up for sale. We know from another source that this was an exaggeration but nevertheless he did have many hundreds.

Activity around the orchards began in earnest towards the middle of June when the nuts were swelling and needing thinning. There were traditional dates for this, which in Surrey usually ran from June 12th to St. Swithin's Day, July 15th. Thinning was achieved by beating the branches with long poles of Ash up to fifteen feet long for the tallest reach but shorter Hazel ones for the lower boughs. In 1557, when the royal palace of Nonsuch was in decline, there was a dispute over ownership of the crop and the rival factions turned their poles on each other!

Beating the trees to promote good harvests is a practice that was probably introduced by the Romans, since the earliest reference traced is ancient Greek. It's mentioned in *Æsop's Fables*, compiled by Babrios in the Alexandrian age. Æsop himself was a Phrygian slave working about 570 BC and wrote:-

As the nuts fell during beating so they were gathered up, and each was pierced with a needle. Often this was children's work. Should the needle pass through then the kernel had not yet begun to harden and the nut would pickle successfully for winter use (source of protein, vitamin C and the vinegar was used as a gargle against sore throats etc.). Should the needle hit a kernel then the fruit needed using straight away, either sold as a good cash crop, or, mashed for the oil (as polish, lubricant, for cooking, reduced as a 'butter', burnt in oil lamps, etc.) and the remaining mash or *lees* or *marc* became pig food. No part of the Walnut tree was useless or waste. The remaining nuts were left on the tree to ripen for an autumn harvest.

"A woman, a dog and a Walnut tree,
The more you beat 'em the better they be."

Sometimes the dog is a spaniel or an ass and the woman is a wife but the important point is that beating breaks off the brittle Walnut twigs and thereby promotes fruiting spurs for next year's harvest. The last time (traced so far) that this beating was performed on an orchard scale, in Surrey, was in Staines in 1943. Not everyone believes in beating! Back in the 17th century John Evelyn reported: *"In Italy they arm the tops of long poles with nails and iron for the purpose, and believe the beating improves the tree; which I no more believe, than I do that discipline would reform a perverse shrew."*

There is an alternative interpretation whereby the *trunk* is beaten in midwinter and in 1970 a lady at Kingston-upon-Thames lost patience with her mature tree that did not fruit and gave it a good thrashing one night, after dark. It fruited next year! That might well be coincidence as it is usually thought that such beating needs to be performed on young trees so that the bark is still so thin that the cambium beneath gets bruised. That shocks the tree into fearing death and it promptly tries to reproduce.

The demise of the great orchards came with twofold developments for the timber. One was for furniture as architecture produced better housing and so English Walnut became important from about 1600-1720. During the 1690s French Walnut began to supersede it, being more reliable for construction work, and then from the 1720s the Virginian Walnut took over. This was from a different tree (*J. nigra*) which was more straight-grained but less figured, but this mattered less when it was to be disguised as a poor man's Mahogany, which ultimately took over.

The second development came also from America: the War of Independence. Suddenly there was an increased demand for firearms and the best timber for rifle stocks is Walnut - strong, shock absorbent, readily shaped and finished, doesn't splinter easily, takes a polish but doesn't become slippery with wet or sweat, feels warm in the cold and cool in the heat - oh it's wonderful stuff! Down came the orchards and off went the timber to the gunsmiths in London. At least one family of gunsmiths made enough money to move out of London and build a 'goodly' house in Surrey. Of course, not all the trees went to the American war but then we had bother with Napoleon (1793-1815) and a lot more were felled. The south chapel of Cobham Parish Church is floored with converted rifle stocks.

ELDER

Sambucus nigra L.

Running back to the heathlands from the banks of the River Wey is the village of Elstead (illustrated). Back in 1128 that was spelt *Ellenstede* - the homesteads dedicated to *Ellen*, the spirit of the Elder tree. At least, she was Ellen to the Saxons, in the south, but to the northern peoples she was *Hylda* and where the cultures merged so Hylda and Ellen become Elder.

Ellen isn't the only old pagan spirit perpetuated in South West Surrey. Thor of Thursday fame gave rise to the next village of Thursley, while at Godalming there's Tuesley, named after Tiw of Tuesday fame and also Eashing of the Ash tree spirit called Aesc or Ask.

Ellen was some sort of mother goddess of protection but little is known for certain about beliefs in tree spirits since the early Christians worked so hard to erase all memory of them. That took a very long time. Even in the 11th century, nearly 400 years after the founding of Chertsey Abbey, King Cnut decided to ban all tree worship with the law of the land. That's enough to tell us the practices were still widespread. Ellen must have been one of their prime targets since any mother figure would be a direct rival to the Blessed Virgin Mary. Consequently Ellen's tree, the Elder, is the only tree in Christendom cursed *twice*, in the name of God, by the Christians, in attempts to turn people away from it. They said it was once a great forest tree that gave the timber to make Christ's Cross and thereby invoked God's displeasure. He cursed it. Never again would it grow to such stature. He shrivelled up its luscious fruits to little berries with poison in the pips and He made it stink. The drooping tree still hangs its head in shame. The other curse was that Judas hanged himself from an Elder, which having supported the traitor, was duly cursed in the aforementioned ways, except that the drooping boughs are not just from shame but are bent from the weight of Judas.

None of these ploys was fully effective. The Puritans promoted the idea that Ellen was a witch to deter people from being seen going through any of the Elder tree rituals. Since the 17th century was a prime time for 'witch hunts' and burnings this was much more of a deterrent so even today many of the witch associations are still well known. Nevertheless, right into the 20th century, people were still planting Elders for protection. They can still be seen at the bottom of country gardens where they safeguarded the privy, or outside doors and windows to deter evil from entering. People still believe it is 'unlucky' to cut Elder without asking it first and in 1995 it was still possible to talk to people who go through the prescribed asking ritual. Whoever cut the underwood on part of Bookham Common in 1985 left every piece of Elder untouched, from mature stools right down to thin-stemmed saplings of only a couple of years growth.

Elder must not be burned either and from Alfold comes (mid 20th century) the tale that villagers spotted Elder in the faggots waiting to go into a wood-burning bread oven whereupon they had the baker remove all the Elder for fear it would put evil in the bread. At Cobham in 1985 the last of the village bakehouses was due for demolition and the main bakehouse was found to have Elders growing all round it whereas the outhouses and fence-sides did not, implying these Elders were planted, rather than having been bird-sown from the gutters above.

The protectiveness of Elder has been vindicated by modern science. We now know the tree produces narcotic compounds, hence the smell, and the multitude of herbal uses. This compound has been demonstrated to be fly-repellent, to the larger disease- spreading flies (small ones pollinate the tree) and so it was wise indeed to plant Elders around dairies, bakeries, privies, kitchen doors and windows and to leave them growing by the midden.

For a fuller story of the Elder see: Chris Howkins,
Elder - Mother Tree of Protection, ISBN 0 9519348 9 9

MAPLES

Acer spp.

A summer wander in Norbury Park can introduce the sharp-eyed to tall mature Field Maples *(Acer campestre)* of which there are not a great many in Surrey. Some more grow on the Hog's Back behind Seale but mostly they are to be found in hedges where they have been topped and cut about. Parting the sprays often reveals a massive bole to testify to their age and to the age of the hedge. Sadly, many people mistake their wavy leaves for Oak and pass them by. Red leaf-stems and galls can highlight the difference in summer but it's the stunning gold of autumn that is unmistakeable.

Similarities with Oak are reflected in its English names, such as Cat Oak and Dog Oak. The latter is an oddity as most 'dog' names refer to plants that were considered useless or inferior whereas this tree's timber has always been prized. Sharp-eyed Saxons had it sorted out from the Oak and in those days there were longer names for it - *Mapletreow, Mapulder and Mapledorn* which during Norman times became *Mapletree* or *Maplintree*. It's not till the 14th century that the familiar short name 'maple' came into use, for which the earliest record is by the poet Geoffrey Chaucer.

There is only one place of significance in Surrey named after the tree and that's the district of Ewhurst called *Mapledrakes*. Back in 1241 the spelling was *Mapledresshe*. They would grow well in the heavy clay of Ewhurst, just as they like the chalk in the places noted above. We'll never know for what exactly those early people at Ewhurst valued the tree but it would almost certainly have been for a timber product. The graining is beautiful and a wood-turner can cut goblets so thin that the wood is all but transparent yet it still has that famous patterning of grain. This is what the Saxons used for making their harps (excavated from Taplow, Berks; and Sutton Hoo, Suffolk) while in later times it was used for making the

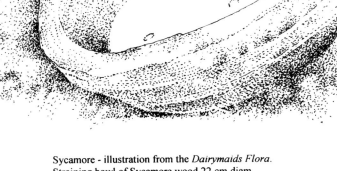

Sycamore - illustration from the *Dairymaids Flora*.
Straining bowl of Sycamore wood 22 cm diam.

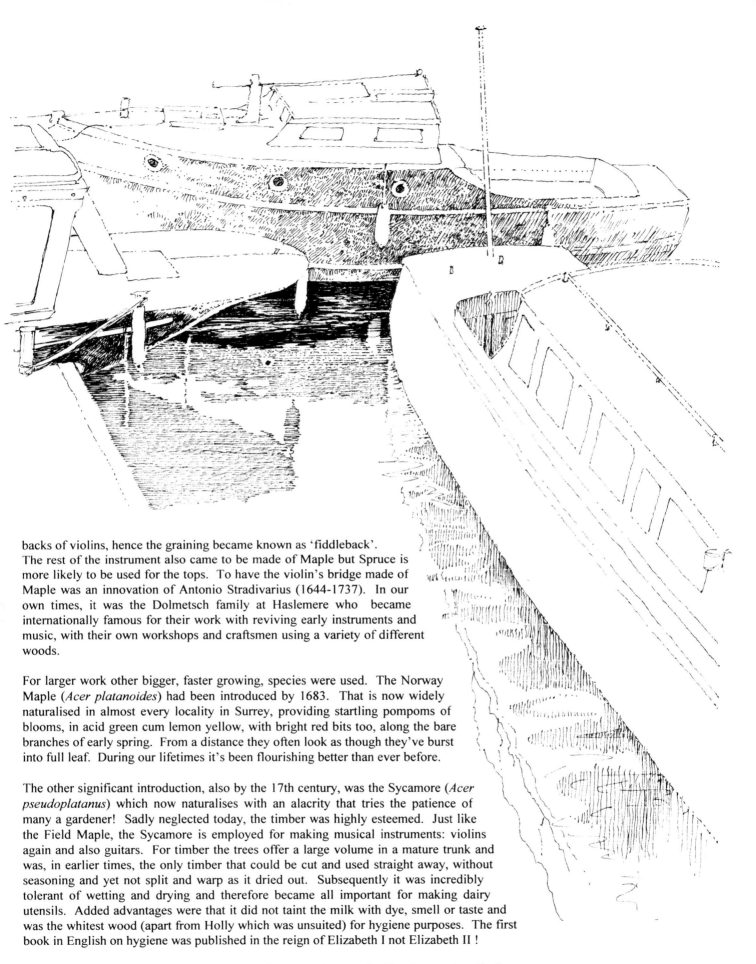

backs of violins, hence the graining became known as 'fiddleback'.
The rest of the instrument also came to be made of Maple but Spruce is
more likely to be used for the tops. To have the violin's bridge made of
Maple was an innovation of Antonio Stradivarius (1644-1737). In our
own times, it was the Dolmetsch family at Haslemere who became
internationally famous for their work with reviving early instruments and
music, with their own workshops and craftsmen using a variety of different
woods.

For larger work other bigger, faster growing, species were used. The Norway
Maple (*Acer platanoides*) had been introduced by 1683. That is now widely
naturalised in almost every locality in Surrey, providing startling pompoms of
blooms, in acid green cum lemon yellow, with bright red bits too, along the bare
branches of early spring. From a distance they often look as though they've burst
into full leaf. During our lifetimes it's been flourishing better than ever before.

The other significant introduction, also by the 17th century, was the Sycamore (*Acer
pseudoplatanus*) which now naturalises with an alacrity that tries the patience of
many a gardener! Sadly neglected today, the timber was highly esteemed. Just like
the Field Maple, the Sycamore is employed for making musical instruments: violins
again and also guitars. For timber the trees offer a large volume in a mature trunk and
was, in earlier times, the only timber that could be cut and used straight away, without
seasoning and yet not split and warp as it dried out. Subsequently it was incredibly
tolerant of wetting and drying and therefore became all important for making dairy
utensils. Added advantages were that it did not taint the milk with dye, smell or taste and
was the whitest wood (apart from Holly which was unsuited) for hygiene purposes. The first
book in English on hygiene was published in the reign of Elizabeth I not Elizabeth II !

For timber purposes these three species have been supplemented with others, primarily from
North America. The best known gave rise to the famous maple-leaf emblem of Canada,
which is to be found frequently in Surrey as part of commemorations of the many links with
Canada during the Second World War. To take one example, they occur on the banner of the

Women's Institute at Sutton Green. The most important of these New World Acers is the source of maple syrup, *Acer saccharum*. Another source of syrup is *Acer saccharinum* and that can be seen on the west side of Woking's 'Turnoak Roundabout' (A320), together with other interesting trees, from when this was a corner of the nursery fields of the famous Jackman's Nursery. In all, there are some 150 species of Acer in cultivation and for one of the rarities there's a mature avenue of *Acer schwerdern* planted beside the B2128 Guildford Road as it becomes the High Street at Cranleigh. These came from E. L. Rowcliffe of Hall Place Estates and are planted for their ornamental value. In this category the finest and best known are of course the small Acers from the Far East, sold as 'Japanese Maples' even though some come from China as well as Japan. Wherever their origins, it's the blaze of autumn colour that makes them particularly famous and it was to create this splendour that they were included in the creation of Winkworth Arboretum (National Trust) on a hillside at Hascombe.

Most of the species grown for timber arrive as timber, rather than being home-grown, and to represent this aspect of *'trees and people'* visits were made to Michael Dennett - a master craftsman who loves the contrast between the beautiful pale Canadian Maple timbers and the rich red of tropical Mahogany. These he crafts together to produce the traditional river boats of the Thames, from his boathouse on the Chertsey bank. This he's been doing all his working life from leaving school and is now one of the last survivors of the days when the Surrey Thames was thick with boatyards and craftsmen. Thankfully his son has caught his passion, been his apprentice, and will continue the craftsmanship.

He doesn't need to advertise in the modern way. Passing boaters spot the 'waiting list' bobbing in the mooring space outside the boathouse and realise this is somewhere special - *"Oh it's the variety that acts as an advert; it changes out there every week."* Sometimes they're grey rotting hulks but all were once richly coloured craft, with shining glass and polished metalwork, fit for any Edwardian regatta. Michael Dennett, with his background knowledge and working experience who knows it's possible to get them back into that state - and he's got the skills to do it. This is the challenge he relishes most but takes great satisfaction in any work done well. Sometimes boats only need repairing, like one of the Royal barges under covers when the drawings were made for this book. Others need varying degrees of restoration while those rotting hulks usually demand re-creation. From time to time this gives the opportunity to change the scale, as was the case with a Thames skiff that was particularly impressive on an earlier visit. The skill here of course is to ensure that it still floats and steers properly but that, he says, is the ultimate test with any of the work - *"At the end of the day it's got to work, got to float; it's not just ornament."* This is possible from his knowledge of the evolution of the boats and their craftsmanship. He looks at a Thames skiff and knows the design is over 200 years old, that once they were used as Thames ferries before being scaled down for pleasure boats and then reduced again for racing boats and he understands the modifications that were involved at each transition so that he can work in any time period he wants.

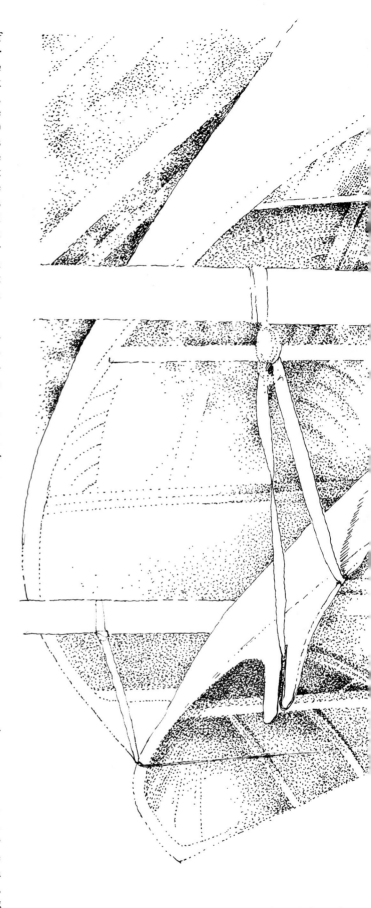

Mr. Michael Dennett beneath the craft suspended from the roof of his boathouse. 1998

A variety of timbers are used. There's Brazilian Cedar, Douglas Fir, English Oak and Ash, Canadian Maple (*"very hard wood - beautiful for contrast"*), African Iroko and Teak from farms in Java. These tropical hardwoods (from renewable resources) are indeed hard, and difficult to work, but that also makes them suitably durable. The English Oak arrives 'green' (unseasoned) and is soaked in the Thames till it sinks and then it's ready for steam-bending, perhaps for the ribs in another Thames skiff.

At the time of the 1998 visit there were craft hanging upside down from the roof of the boathouse, ready to be worked, while bobbing in the Thames outside was a steam boat, over a hundred years old, is also awaiting treatment. Upturned on the bank was a Thames canoe of a design that came originally from the USA. It's a wreck so Michael Dennett planned to recreate it. Whether it's a big boat or a little boat the challenge is the same - crafting together beauty and function with durability.

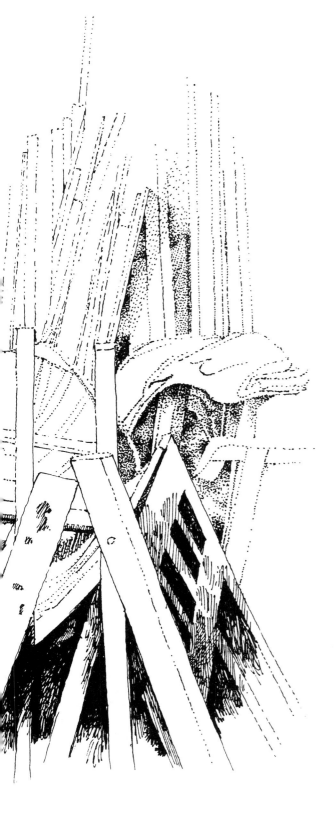

Michael Dennett
with his Thames skiff
1990

LIMES

Tilia spp.and hybrids

Drip, drip, drip, and you know you've parked your car in the wrong place, under a Lime tree, (is that why it's now called the Traffic Warden Tree?). Aphids thrive in the foliage and exude gallons of sticky honeydew, unless the tree is *Tilia x euchora*, the Caucasian Lime, which is now the hybrid preferred for street planting. It can also be seen as an avenue along the ridge in Farnham Park.

There are about 45 species in the genus, in two main groups, and they hybridize freely, making identification difficult for even the experts. To most of the people who made the records of our cultural history a Lime tree was simply a Lime tree. For the last few hundred years they have been so popular that they are now one of the commonest planted trees, usually the Hybrid Lime, *Tilia x vulgaris*. Avenues have always been popular, and still are - there's a young one across Pirbright village green, glorious in its autumn gold and just as beautiful, if more subtle, in its soft fresh green of unfurling spring. There is something very English about them and many were used to fulfil the plans of the 'Garden City' ideal, including the early version at Bedford Park, Chiswick. The most important Lime, in the prehistoric history of our landscape, was the Small-leaved Lime, *Tilia cordata* Miller, which had become scarce by historic times and remains so today. It flourished 3,000-5,000 BC and it is now argued, controversially, that it may have dominated sandy areas and have disappeared with the clearances that gave rise to the heathlands. Thus it might have given rise to the name Blindley Heath, being *lind* or Lime, *leach* or clearing.

Prehistoric peoples would have harvested it eagerly. Not only is it the lightest European wood but it makes excellent firewood, and charcoal for fueling the development of metallurgy. It coppices well as a renewable resource and at some very early date the inner bark was discovered to make the best rope. Peeled off in strips, these were then soaked in water for 4-6 weeks until micro-organisms made it possible to separate the 10-12 inner layers which could then be twisted into rope. This was re-enacted for an experiment to demonstrate ways in which the great stones could have been manoeuvered into place at Stonehenge. That really showed how strong the ropes were. Gardeners have their own version. Remember when Chrysants. and tomatoes were tied with a buff 'raffia' called *bass*? Well, that's the same inner fibres, from America where they call Lime trees *Basswoods*. Apparently you can still buy it.

When the prehistoric peoples came to building their homes they might well have thatched over Lime rafters, as the coppice poles can be long and straight, and the thatch tied down with Lime fibre rope. This suggestion has arisen out of the persistence for using Lime spars for thatching ricks, which is otherwise difficult to explain. Spars three feet long were used for hay ricks and four feet long for corn ricks. As Lime became rarer so the rick-masters turned to other trees that produced inch-thick rods: Elm, Willow, Ash and sometimes Maple. Now even the ricks are rarities in the countryside.

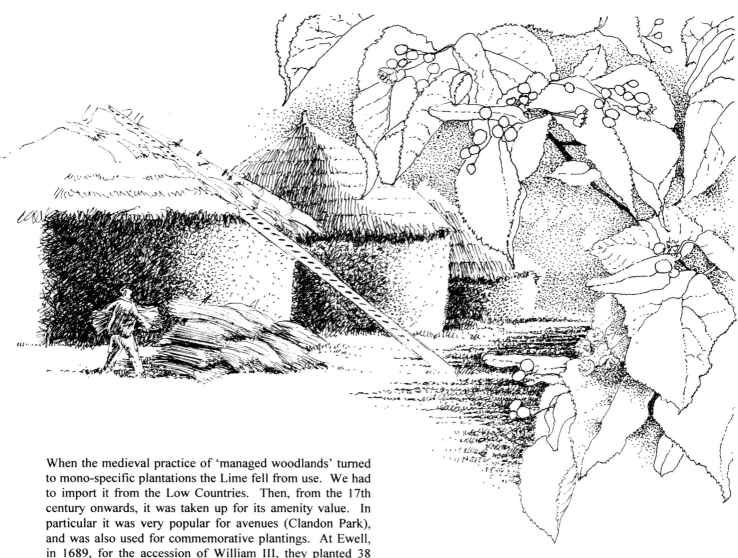

When the medieval practice of 'managed woodlands' turned to mono-specific plantations the Lime fell from use. We had to import it from the Low Countries. Then, from the 17th century onwards, it was taken up for its amenity value. In particular it was very popular for avenues (Clandon Park), and was also used for commemorative plantings. At Ewell, in 1689, for the accession of William III, they planted 38 Limes to represent his age (some survive in The Grove between the High Street and West Street). In 1849, at Elstead, they bought a lime (by the churchyard entrance), to commemorate an outbreak of cholera (see Cedar).

Usage for the timber has never died out completely, for this became the chosen medium of the decorative woodcarvers for the great houses. It is fairly readily cut and has a very even grain with no bold distinction between sapwood and heartwood. Without rival, the greatest master of this was Grinling Gibbons. He was introduced to the Royal Court by John Evelyn, says John Evelyn. Thus we have grand examples of his work at some of the royal houses. That at Hampton Court Palace was destroyed in part by the 1986 fire, including a seven foot 'drop'. One person in the world was known to have the skill with which to re-create it. He was David Esterly, from America, who achieved just that and stunned the experts with his quality. Some ten years on and another fire, at Windsor Castle, destroyed some of the limewood 'trophies' - "miraculous objects, carved from limewood boards usually no more than three-quarters of an inch thick but with a vitality, precision and three dimensional quality that totally belies their actual depth," reported the Sunday Telegraph Magazine (16-11-1998) after restoration was complete. These trophies were re-created by Dick Reid. Even with his skill his practice piece of two square inches, for the purposes of estimating costs, totalled £3,370. The total contract came to £511,576.

That's all a far cry from the days in the Second World War when Lime was used for making coffins in Surrey. One of the workmen described this during the tea-break at a talk in 1992. These are the people who reveal the 'tricks of the trade' that the documents leave concealed. Lime planks, he said, must not be stacked for seasoning without gaps between them, otherwise they all stick together. Grinling Gibbons' timber merchants must have known that.

Finally, Limes are the only trees in Surrey to be used whole for herbal medicine. They were planted around asylums once it became known that the scent of the blossom has a calming, mildly sedative affect upon the nervous system. The county's great mental hospitals have gone in recent years but often the trees remain, as at Brookwood. Limes are important medicinal trees - their action is gentle and therefore suitable as relaxants for children with nervous irritability. They are a mild tranquilizer and help induce sleep. Also they help the heart and circulation where conditions are affected by anxiety and tension. In France this is the most popular of all the herbal teas and when given to American children recovering from 'flu' they did better than those on antibiotics. Anyone following recipes for making their own should remember not to steep for many minutes but infuse quickly and not to use ageing blossoms.

MEDLAR

Mespilus germanica L

This is a beautiful tree for the garden. Although it can grow up to 25ft high it is usually about the stature of a spreading Apple tree. It can grow just as delightfully crooked but often becomes multi-trunked. In late spring and early summer the firm green shoots are dotted all over with single white blossoms, about an inch across. These develop through the summer into weird pear-shaped fruits with leafy bracts circling the open top. Come autumn and the leaves put on a vibrant colourful display, until they and the fruits fall. Leave the fruits on the ground or where Jack Frost can walk across them. Once 'bletted' by the ice they are then soft and ready to eat. Not everyone in the past has liked them but today few have even heard of them as the tree has become rare. There's one open to public view at Loseley.

The drawing was made from a beautiful multi-trunked one in a private garden in Weybridge. They were tasted at the same time - very sweet, like a cross between soft toffee and fudge, textured like sugar crystals in fudge. It was not very impressive, at first, but leaves you wanting more and in no time at all they were deemed quite delicious! This was definitely a treat to be repeated at the next opportunity!

Readers should be warned that not everyone gets so enthusiastic! It's your bowels you see! Medlars are an 'opener' and through the Middle Ages were given the pertinent name of *open-arse*, as in Chaucer's Canterbury Tales. Throughout this period Medlars were a very important fruit when there was a scarcity of foods that were naturally sweet, let alone laxative. For whatever reason they were recommended to all monasteries in a famous list by Charlemagne in AD 800. It's not until c.1270 that we get the earliest English reference, when the gardener monks at Westminster Abbey were directed to provide these fruits for the monastery. Perhaps they were grown on one of their Surrey manors, such as Pyrford.

The usual practice was to eat them after a meal, in later times with port wine, as a digestive aid. They were high status too, being among gifts given to Henry VIII. Over in France the monarch was always offered them on visits to Orléans, which was famed for its Medlars and in particular for a preserve they made called 'cotignac'. Even Jeanne D'Arc was given this as her first present when she triumphantly entered the city. In England, since Tudor times, Medlars have dwindled very much from favour, partly perhaps, because none of the gardening book writers got at all excited about them. Even the tree lacks enthusiasm for naturalising in Surrey; there are only a couple of wild ones. It prefers Kent and Sussex.

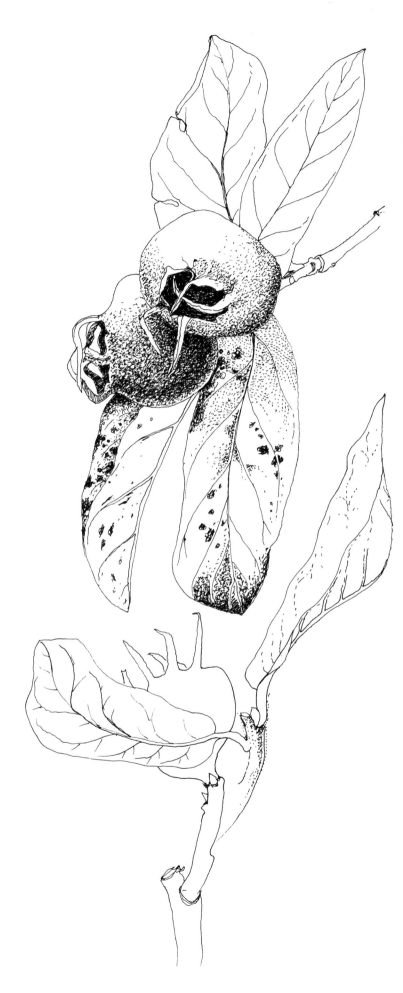

MULBERRIES

White Mulberry - Morus alba L
Black Mulberry - Morus nigra L

There used to be a fine old Mulberry hanging over the wall into the northern end of Haslemere High Street. Children called it the 'raspberry tree' from the similarity of its fruits with which it carpeted the pavement every summer. It's gone now, like so many others in Surrey, leaving behind names like 'Mulberry House', Mulberry Cottage', and 'Mulberry End' - their gardens now bereft of these beautiful trees.

Above - Loseley House

Mulberries were definitely grown here by the Romans; there are over a hundred records, and these would have been the Black Mulberry. Popular statements that the tree was introduced about 1500 are wrong and so this includes that entrenched claim by Syon House in London that the first was planted there in 1548. Where the tree came from originally is not known; some think it came from S. E. Europe, in which case it has been extinct in the wild for a long time, while others favour it coming along the trade routes from the East.

Bearing in mind it is hardy enough to survive British winters it would be amazing if the treee was not here in the Middle Ages since it is mentioned several times in the Bible and that was always enough to enhance the status of any tree. There are indeed medieval records indicating that it persisted after Roman times. For example the monks at Canterbury Cathedral Priory must have had them for Gerald of Wales during his 12th century visit much enjoyed supping the wine made from the fruit. Modern scholarship has demoted some of the Bible references, such as *"...and come upon them, over against the mulberry trees. And let it be when thou hearest the sound of a going in the tops of the mulberry trees, that then shalt thou bestir thyselves."* *(2 Sam. 5, 23-4, repeated in 1 Ch. 14, 14-15; AV)* because that implies rustling and

so is believed now to refer to a Poplar, *Populus euphratica*. More reliable references to the Mulberry are to the *sycamine*, as *"and the Lord said, If ye hat faith as a grain of mustard seed, ye might say unto this sycamine tree, Be thou plucked up by the root, and be thou planted in the sea, and it should obey you."* *(Luke 17, 6; AV)* Furthermore, early translations used 'silk' where 'linen' was intended and this has been corrected in later versions. Silk was not produced by the Jews until c.600 BC and does not get a Bible reference until Ezekiel (c.200 BC). By this time the White Mulberry, food of silkworms, had obviously reached the Middle East, from it's native E. and S. E. Asia. It arrived in Europe by the 12th century but when it reached England isn't known.

Coxes Lock
1982

Although we were *weaving* silk
by the 15th century that does
not mean it was home-produced
- they had to overcome the
problem of the climate being too
cold for the silk worms. The value of
silk was such that the financial return was
too great to resist, and so, in November 1609
the Lord Lieutenants of all the counties received
a letter from His Majesty King James I, forewarning
them that come the following March a thousand
Mulberry trees would be delivered to each county town.
These were to be sold off at three farthings each or six
shillings a hundred, to be grown on as silkworm food for an
English silk industry. He set an example with plantings at
Buckingham Palace but also in Surrey at Oatlands Palace.
This can be seen in the background of the portait of his
queen, Anne of Denmark, in the Queen's Collection (print in
Weybridge Museum) and the Mulberry orchard can be seen
showing over the wall to the right. In 1630 the famous royal
gardener John Tradescant the Elder was appointed *Keeper of
His Majesty's Gardens, Vines and Silkworms at Oatlands.*
There is a tradition that the nearby mill at Coxes Lock was
used as a silk mill at one time. This has been much debated,
and if it happened at all, must have been a very short-lived
enterprise, as indeed was King James's.

The Palace was destroyed by order of the Puritan Parliament
and the site has since been built on, including St. Maur's
Convent where the Mulberry trees in the grounds of are
claimed to be three survivors from King James's plantings.
The nearest thing to a royal palace still standing in Surrey is
Loseley House near Guildford (open to visitors), which has
had many royal visits. It was built (1561-9) for the More
family, (whose descendants live there still) and they took the
Mulberry tree name *Morus* as their rebus which can be seen
along the cornices with their motto *morus barde moriens -
morem cito moriturum* - the Mulberry dies slowly - though
its fruit dies soon. Outside is a Mulberry tree reputedly
planted by Elizabeth I and another by Queen Mary in 1932.

TALE FROM
UNDER A MULBERRY TREE

A Greek story has been well-known in England for as nearly as long as the Black Mulberry, since the story of Pyramus and Thisbe was adapted by Skakespeare into *A Midsummer Night's Dream.*

Pyramus fell in love with Thisbe, the girl next door, but she was a Babylonian girl so their parents would not let them marry. They talked to each other through a hole in the garden wall. On one occasion they agreed to meet at Ninus' tomb. Thisbe arrived first and on hearing the roar of a lion, fled in fright, dropping her garment as she went. The lion savaged it. When Pyramus arrived he concluded that the lion had eaten Thisbe. Mortified, he stabbed himself. Thisbe returned to find Pyramus dead, and so she also stabbed herself.

(Ovid, Metamorphoses, IV)

This all happened under a Mulberry tree and it was their blood that supposedly gave the red colour to the fruits.

WEATHER LORE

"The Mulberry is accounted of all other trees the wisest, because he never blossometh till all cold weather be quite fast: so that whensoever you see the mulberry begin to spring you maybe sure that winter is at an end."

***

When the mulberry has shown green leaf, there will be no more frost.

***

When the mulberry tree grows green,
the last of winter's frosts you've seen.

APPLES

Malus domestica Borkh
Malus sylvestris (L.) Miller

As summertime ripens towards autumn so the crab apples glow in green and gold and red along the drooping branches, ready to fall among the leaves and weeds below. The trees show up best in blossom time, in whites and pinks, when all the wild apple trees along the roadsides draw attention to themselves. They've grown from the pips in apple cores tossed from car windows. Later on their fruits bear little resemblance to the apples that were bought in the shops because they do not come 'true' from seed. They 'revert' to the characteristics in their parentage, hence all the variety in pattern of growth as well as in the colour of their blossom and fruits. These are now grouped as *Malus domestica* as opposed to the true wild Crab Apple, *Malus sylvestris* but telling the difference can be very difficult unless the branches have the thorns of the true Wild Crab. To most people through the ages they were simply apples. From earliest times they have been sacred or at the very least, considered to be the food of the soul, particularly for the journey from the body to the next world.

In early times it was the largest edible fruit and one that would keep for many weeks; months, if cut into rings and smoked over the fire. Nevertheless, they can be very sour indeed so people have always had a sharp eye for a variant that was bigger and sweeter. Dotted around Surrey, as with other counties, there have been enthusiasts who worked at breeding improved strains. Over forty cultivars are believed to have been of Surrey origin. Many of these are preserved in the National Fruit Collection from where communities can arrange to get rooted stock from which to grow their own local speciality. These often bearing the name of their origins, such as the *Addlestone Pippin, Albury Park Nonsuch, Byfleet Seedling, Claygate Pearmain, Cleeve, Egham Seedling, Mickleham Pearmain, Nutfield Beauty, Orange Silvermere Seedling* and the *Surrey Flat-cap.*

The names of other apples commemorate those Surrey people who raised them: *Carswell's Orange* by J. W. Carswell at Ashtead from seed sown in 1938 and *Carswell's Honeydew* in 1939; *Wadey's Seedling* by W. J. Wadey at Caterham in 1919; *Balchin's Pearmain* by a Mr. Balchin at Dorking some time before 1884. *Robert Jordan* was exhibited in 1903 by the man of that name from Godalming; *Herbert's Prolific* by a Mr. Herbert of Redhill just prior to 1918; *Braddick's Nonpareil* by John Braddick of Thames Ditton; *Harrison's Seedling* by a Mr. Harrison of Oatlands, while *Mary Green* was named and promoted by D. E. Green of Send just as *Harry Pring* raised the apple that bears his name, at Leatherhead, from where it was introduced onto the market by W. Peters, soon to be followed by *William Peters.*

Others were found by chance such as *The Skeet's Pearmain* found by Mr. Skeet in the garden of the Running Horses pub in Mickleham or *Margaret Taylor* which was found in a garden hedge at Witley by F. E. Taylor. The *Hannan Seedling*, was raised from a pip out of an Australian apple, in 1928 by Mrs I. Hannan at Walton-on-Thames.

Byfleet holds the record for the greatest number from one source (excluding the work of The Royal Horticultural Society's garden at Wisley, associated one way or another with such cultivars as *Coloured Grieve, Crimson Cottenham, Millicent Barnes Sport,* and *Summer Blenheim*). It was at Byfleet's West Hall that Mr Frederick Cornelius Stoop employed George Carpenter as his head gardener, and apart from being a quality gardener in general, George Carpenter had a keen interest in fruit, especially apples and pears. His breeding stock was trained into arched tunnels, which still survive in part among the office car parks at West Hall (illus). Six of his apples are recorded in the National Fruit Register: *Byfleet Seedling*, raised in 1915, went to the National Trials in 1931 where *Victory* had been received in 1923, followed by *Comrade* and *Ye Old Peasgood* in 1932; *Shoesmith* began trials in 1954 but the only reference to *Utility* is for being first exhibited in 1930.

All manner of memories survive of Stoop and Carpenter. The former was a local benefactor, giving Byfleet its village hall for example, but remembered by one lady as *"a little Dutch tyrant. VERY wealthy - from commerce, you know; he was not out of the top drawer - nothing but a shop-keeper really."* The same person remembered Stoop's wife as *"a plump comfortable lady, very pleasant, Scottish I think - like today's Queen Mother. She was fair skinned - gave an impression of pinkness. Don't know how she came to be married to that dictatorial fussy little man - they put on an annual garden party for their friends; thought they were the BEST people but my mother said they weren't the BEST - she'd worked for the BEST."*

82

All manner of memories survive of Stoop and Carpenter. The former was a local benefactor, giving Byfleet its village hall for example, but remembered by one lady as *"a little Dutch tyrant. VERY wealthy - from commerce, you know; he was not out of the top drawer - nothing but a shop keeper really."* The same person remembered Stoop's wife as *"a plump comfortable lady, very pleasant, Scottish I think - like today's Queen Mother. She was fair skinned - gave an impression of pinkness. Don't know how she came to be married to that dictatorial fussy little man - they put on an annual garden party for their friends; thought they were the BEST people but my mother said they weren't the BEST she'd worked for the BEST."*

Carpenter is remembered, *"with an impressive beard and moustache, keen on Christian virtues - truth and honesty and all that - very forthright man he was ; 'spected other men to be the same. He was a God-fearing man; always went to church on Sundays* [Byfleet parish church; sang in the choir]. *They were what you'd call old-fashioned Christians. He was very Victorian, very strict."* From his house in the midst of the grounds of West Hall he ruled his team: second gardener, lawnsman, greenhouse gardener, hot-house gardener, vegetable gardener, and drives man. Those that pleased him were invited with their children to tea on Sunday, when Carpenter played with the children and is remembered warmly in this respect, except when he smothered little faces with his beard in order to kiss them. He had no children of his own. Then once a year, for Byfleet's 'Parish Day' he'd put on a display in the flower show tent - *"a rather modest display - so as not to deter other villagers."*

Sadly the Surrey apple orchards have nearly dwindled away completely, from the days when nearly all the farms made their own cider for their workers. Perhaps only one farm retains its old cider press and the words of the Wassailing songs are but dead words preserved on a page.

SWEET CHESTNUT

Castanea sativa Miller

This is the tree, back in 1769, that started off an interest in the history of ecology - a theme which features considerably in a book like this. The tree provoked correspondence with the Royal Society as to whether or not it was a native. There are still writers who say that it is but archaeologists have found no evidence for its presence before Roman times. In particular there is no preserved pollen. The very few pieces of wood may either be from imported items or be pieces of Oak which can be very similar unless the wood shows clear medullary rays.

With the coming of the Romans the records begin. That is hardly surprising since they knew it well from its homeland in southern Europe and knew how to exploit its virtues, particularly the nuts for food. They must have been pleased to discover the tree grew well here and would naturalise. Indeed England is the only country in N. W. Europe where these trees were introduced and did take to the wild. Thus our wild Surrey Chestnuts are very special.

Jackdaws are the only birds which have learnt to break open the fruits while they are still on the tree.

We have plenty of Sweet Chestnut trees that were originally planted, usually in coppices, from when the 17th century landowners realised they would give a good financial return, especially on poor sandy soils. Landowners were being told by writers such as John Evelyn that the stools could be cropped every eight years. So they can but only for smallish rods. Long poles, for the hop fields etc. require a longer rotation, from 12-18 years, with sixteen being very workable on most sites. An acre of land can carry 590 stools and if these are spaced eight feet apart will yield some 2,500 poles but obviously the working practices varied considerably. Only a few ancient Chestnuts remain in Surrey from those early days but in the 19th century there was fresh interest in the tree and from this period there are many remaining coppices. Sadly, they are often overgrown and neglected today, despite there still being a ready market for several of the Chestnut coppice products. They are the only coppice products to be covered by the British Standards regulations.

Chestnut makes up over half of the coppices in Southern England. Most are in Kent but Surrey has its share, especially among the sandstone hills of the S. W. corner, around Hambledon and Hascombe, and again on the Haslemere/Hindhead Hills. These run into the Hampshire countryside, beyond Farnham and over the Sussex border as the Blackdown and Marley hills, with the outlier of Telegraph Hill further south beyond Fernhurst.

These were all planted for their wood rather than for nuts which have not been the prime concern in this country. In particular, this crop was promoted in parallel with an expanding population and with it the development of commercial brewing. Even small towns like Reigate and Horley had their own breweries. Hundreds of thousands of acres of the countryside were given over to hop fields and with that came an enormous demand for hop poles. This demand took out the longest poles, but the remaining smaller ones all had their markets, ranging from fencing to walking sticks. Surrey had centres for making both: Peasmarsh for the former and Chiddingfold for the latter. The National Health Service walking sticks are still made from Chestnut, at a factory in Gloucestershire.

It was here on the Surrey/Sussex borders that the chestnut-paling fencing industry began, at the very beginning of the 20th century when other woodland crafts were declining. In particular, the hoopers were finding less and less demand for their barrel hoops and the hurdlers were losing out to barbed wire (invented in the USA in the previous century). Both these groups of craftsmen found they could turn readily to cutting fence pales because they could continue to use the same tools, primarily their adze. In due course they changed this for the break-axe, which they found was easier.

The pale-cutters worked in the coppices. Felled poles were riven with the adze or axe into the pales, making up bundles of twenty five, which a good craftsman reckoned to be able to get from a single pole. Working the pole lengths radially produced roughly triangular pales, which are a British speciality - French ones are square. This work was often performed in the lee of a tarpaulin that had been strung up against the wind and rain.

The bundles were sold on, at piecework rates, from the coppices to the work-yards of the fence-makers. These worked in long sheds, over thirty feet long, since that was the maximum length of a roll of English chestnut-paling fencing. Miles and miles of it went to war, to be rolled out as temporary roadways over soft ground. Indeed, to satisfy the war demand the makers at the 'Astolat' works at Peasmarsh, required a whole train, which was loaded up at the former Godalming Goods Station. Then in the 1930s chain-link fencing came on the market and demand fell and with it many of the coppices. More declined by the 1980s with a sharp fall in demand for hop poles, due to the breeding of new stronger strains of hops, requiring fewer acres, and also due to social changes in favour of Continental beers.

As well as coppicing, Chestnut could also be pollarded. This particular pollard stands beside the B3000 just south of Compton village and was just beginning to regenerate in 1996 after recent cutting.

Found more frequently in Surrey are olsa Oak pollards. One of the largest collections in the country is on Ashtead Common.

Split the Chestnut even smaller, to one inch widths, and there are the lathes for lathe-and-plaster walls and ceilings. These lathes were nailed to the beams leaving about a quarter of an inch between them, into which the plaster was pressed and there it will hold if done properly. Today of course, there are modern alternatives but craftsmen still exist who can produce the traditional. They are scattered in small firms around the country where they can normally satisfy demand but it was a different story when it came to restoring Hampton Court Palace after the 1986 fire. So many lathes would be needed that it would not have been possible to hand-craft all of them within the time allowance of the contract. Thus expanded metal was used for the ceiling of the Cartoon Gallery but craftsmen split Chestnut by hand for all the rest, while others devised a modern recipe for the 'traditional' plaster.

Mattresses have changed too. In the 17th century they were sometimes stuffed with Chestnut leaves but Evelyn warns that Beech leaves were better because they did not betray bed-time activities with such loud crackling!

As for the nuts, they do not feature greatly in the social records of Surrey. School Log Books, from Victorian times, such as those for Ottershaw, record school closures in November to enable the children to gather acorns and chestnuts. The Chestnut coppices of Ottershaw Park survive, although overgown, and sections have been bought recently by Runnymede Borough Council and given public access.

Also in Victorian times, when the celebration of Bonfire Night on November 5th was still a legal requirement, there was a fair at Guildford, held on St. Catherine's Hill. It became a focal point of the notorious riots to which these celebrations gave licence. After the 1863 riot the Chief Constable had to explain the apparent lack of police control, and he reported that it had become traditional at the fair for the stall-holders to pelt each other with chestnuts. On this occasion the usual good fun got out of hand and the general public got pelted as well!

HAZEL

Corylus avellana L.

If Chestnuts were not significant for food, Hazel nuts certainly were. Coming ready packaged in their shells for easy and lasting storage, they were an important source of protein, from prehistoric to Edwardian times. By the 20th century though, the usage was in sharp decline.

Fortunately Surrey had thousands of acres of Hazel coppice. These were primarily for charcoal, right through to the end of the Tudor period, to fuel the nation's industrial heartland, which until that time was in the south east. A single forge needed five tons of charcoal every week. That required 120 acres of working coppice. Hazel rods had a multitude of other uses too. The one we see most today is in the timber-framed buildings where Hazel rods provided the wattles for the wattle-and-daub panels between the timber framing. The much larger woven panels, known as hurdles, were in great demand as moveable fences for livestock control. All in all there were some four dozen uses for the coppice products.

It so happened that the stools were not often cut before the Hazel had started fruiting and so there was a bountiful supply of nuts. Grey squirrels (scuggies in Surrey dialect) were not introduced until the 19th century; red squirrels and dormice were not a major threat. Thus every autumn there was the great nut harvest, with robust boys shinning up the tallest poles to bend them over under their weight for everyone else to strip off the nuts. A set day was chosen by the community so that everyone had a fair chance and in Surrey this was usually after 14th September. That date was officially Holy Rood Day or Holy Cross Day, to commemorate the miraculous appearance of Christ's Cross to Constantine. Unofficially it became known as the Day of the Holy Nut, when the nuts were safe, since only the Devil would go nutting on that day. Nobody wanted to be seen to be in league with the Devil. Similarly, nutting on Sundays was considered sinful.

The conclusion of the harvest was celebrated with a church service, on Crack Nut Day, so called because nuts were taken to church and produced at the appropriate moment during the service. They were then cracked open and eaten. The children must have loved it, especially as they may well have had extra nuts passed along from ageing grandparents with few teeth left! Otherwise sections of the congregation must have disappeared down behind their pews to crack open the nuts with their clogs - and then blown the bits off the kernels. There were different rituals in the north country but everywhere there were rituals concerning Hazel as it was one of the most spiritually potent trees. In Surrey the service was saved for Michaelmas Eve, 28th September.

Problems arose towards the end of the 19th century when the authorities tried to enforce compulsory school attendance following the 1870 Education Act. The children were needed for the vital harvest and so the usual solution was to prevail upon the school authorities to grant an official day's closure. Many School Log Books record these but oddly not some of the schools in prime Hazel country. Instead they sometimes had a day off for 'wooding'. This may be a euphemism to disguise the true purpose from the chairman of the local school authorities who would be called upon to sanction the day off. Very often he was an important local landowner, maybe not of an understanding local country origin, who might have thought of this harvest as theft - off his own land! Other landlords tried to restrict their tenants to live off the estate's own corn harvest which, it was stipulated, must be ground in the landlord's mill,
for a price. Nuts might have
been considered an evasion
of this income.

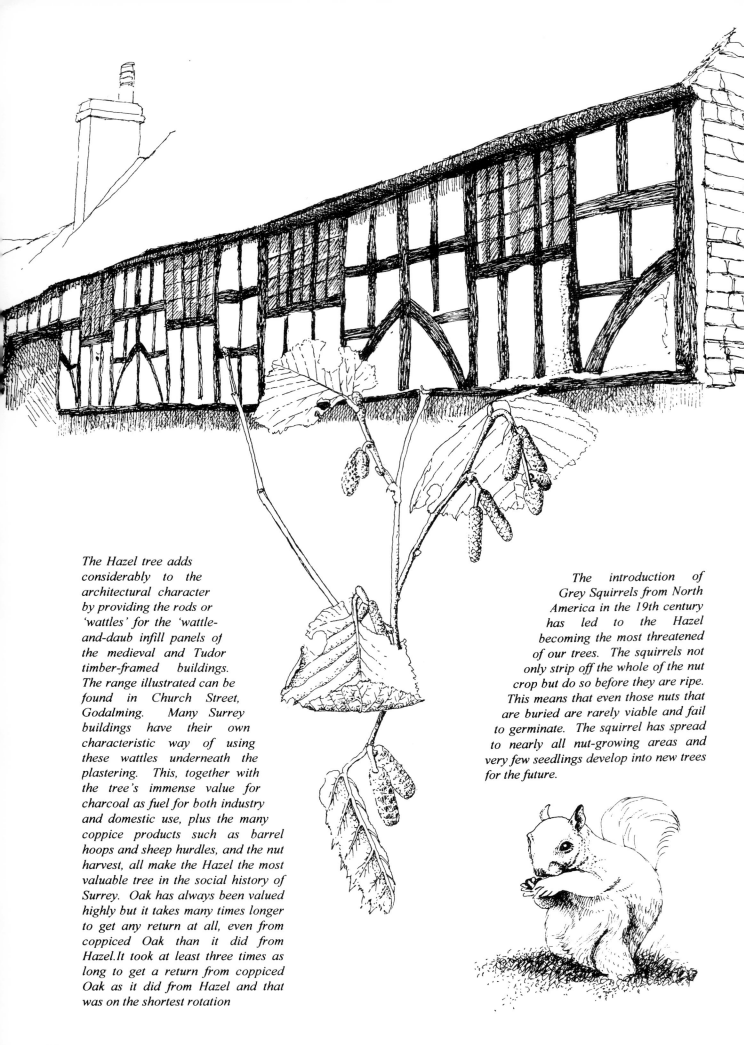

The Hazel tree adds considerably to the architectural character by providing the rods or 'wattles' for the 'wattle-and-daub infill panels of the medieval and Tudor timber-framed buildings. The range illustrated can be found in Church Street, Godalming. Many Surrey buildings have their own characteristic way of using these wattles underneath the plastering. This, together with the tree's immense value for charcoal as fuel for both industry and domestic use, plus the many coppice products such as barrel hoops and sheep hurdles, and the nut harvest, all make the Hazel the most valuable tree in the social history of Surrey. Oak has always been valued highly but it takes many times longer to get any return at all, even from coppiced Oak than it did from Hazel. It took at least three times as long to get a return from coppiced Oak as it did from Hazel and that was on the shortest rotation

The introduction of Grey Squirrels from North America in the 19th century has led to the Hazel becoming the most threatened of our trees. The squirrels not only strip off the whole of the nut crop but do so before they are ripe. This means that even those nuts that are buried are rarely viable and fail to germinate. The squirrel has spread to nearly all nut-growing areas and very few seedlings develop into new trees for the future.

HOLLY

Ilex aquifolium L.

Traditional Christian symbolism has the Holly being the body of Christ. Thus when it is used as a Christmas decoration it should not enter the house until after midnight on Christmas Eve - *"Well, you can't have Jesus arriving before his birthday, can you?"* explained my mother. Similarly no woman must then touch it: *"You can't have a woman touching the body of Jesus. It wouldn't be seemly."* Another problem is what to do with it after Christmas. Some people insist it should be burned (return Jesus to spiritual form?) whereas others insist it should not on any account be burned, so then what do you do with it? Dropping Jesus into the wheelie-bin or the garden shredder doesn't seem quite seemly either! In parts of the Thames valley, such as at Laleham, they believed that begging the church Holly off the vicar and feeding it to the ewes would ensure they gave birth to twin lambs. As the ram had the time of his life before 5th November it seems a bit late on Twelfth Night to initiate such fertility rituals.

The extensive Christmas use makes the Holly the most important native tree in religious usage; the last great survivor of many. In the past its secular uses made it highly prized. Thus when C. P. Johnson wrote his *Useful Plants of Great Britain* in 1862 he reported that *"In England the tree is usually small, rarely found growing to more than the size of a large bush, a circumstance partly to be accounted for by the value of the timber, which caused the larger trees to be felled in old times..."* It has the whitest of British woods although it can be greenish to start with, and this was much used for the white sections in all types of inlay work for furnishings. Surrey Hollies probably went over the Kent border for making the inlays in 'Tunbridge Ware'. This began in the 17th century and lasted until the 1930s.

That wouldn't have taken all the big Hollies though. Another important use was for making the wooden blocks for printing calico. That takes its name from Calicut in India from where it was being imported by the 11th century. By the 12th century it was being printed: it arrived plain and was piece-dyed to give a ground colour over which designs were then printed. This became particularly important in Europe during the 17th and 18th centuries, when it was used for hangings and bed covers and, in England, for ladies'

costume, especially dresses. Holly printing blocks are still used in craft workshops today.

Another reason why there were few big Hollies was because they were eaten. The trees were pollarded to provide winter fodder and the ageing trunks became hollow and useless for the timber merchant. This fodder needed careful nibbling because of the prickles and this stopped the livestock getting mental problems from boredom. Otherwise it was crushed, with a water-worn stone in a wooden trough in counties like Surrey where there was no suitable stone for making the large trough used elsewhere and hammered with a wooden beetle. The foliage can be somewhat toxic in large amounts and so it was mixed in with other fodder such as the hay.

The pollards were known as *hollins* but in many areas this is the local name for the Holly tree anyway. It comes from the Saxon *holegn* and has nothing to do with *holy* as is so often stated. Otherwise it got the name *holm* and led John Evelyn, and countless writers since, to claim that the Hollies on the common gave rise to the name Holmwood south of Dorking. This is not true. The old Court Rolls invariably have Homewood, from when this was the woodland of the home or main farm of the manor. Evelyn also made the same assumption for Vale of Holmsdale, running eastwards to Reigate - a notion published nationally by Johnson two hundred years later and still popular. Certainly there are plenty of Hollies in the district and they may have encouraged the name change. Nationally the Holly ranks eighth, with Lime, in the origin of place names, according to Oliver Rackham's, *History of the Countryside*. Old Holly names in Surrey are scarce but *Holdhurst Farm* at Cranleigh is believed to be one.

There are some good Holly hedges in the county though. One has been remarked upon regularly and that is a massive one, at Pennyhill, Bagshot. It still survives and is indeed truly stunning. Eric Parker described it for his *Surrey Gardens* as *"hand-clipped from soil to top, and measures in length 225 yards. In height it has been cut by the head gardener at Pennyhill to 40 feet over most of its length, but in one place it is nearer 50 feet..........I shall always remember my first view of it, when on a day in June 1952, we stood, my daughter and I, looking out at the hedge in the afternoon sunlight. It stretched the full length of the horizon, a great right-angled part of it higher than the rest, on our right and left, with a long line of pine woods under the sky beyond."*

Hollies
Ottershaw

John Evelyn's famous Holly hedge that was damaged by Peter the Great was not at the family home at Wotton as is sometimes claimed but at Evelyn's personal home at Sayers Court. That was in Deptford, not the Sayers Court at Addlestone. Just up the road from Addlestone, at Ottershaw, are some Holly hedges all about the village and all the more beautiful for having so many variegated ones included. Some have been allowed to grow up into small round-headed trees to make the traditional 'standards' stationed along the lines. These hedges mark the former field boundaries of the nursery lands of the Fletcher family. It was William Fletcher who took over the land c.1852, to be followed by his three sons until the First World War when the nursery covered 105 acres. In other hands it lasted until 1934. The nursery was of some importance (see box). Now that the land has been built over the Holly hedges are a beautiful record of local history. The local council tries to safeguard them and objected to one development proposal in 1997 which was overturned on appeal to the Department of the Environment. That granted permission on condition the trees and hedges be saved - but the developers ripped out 50 feet of Holly hedgerow before they could be stopped - according to a report in the local *Informer* (7-11-1997).

Another historic strip of Holly hedge can be found behind Woking station. It was saved when the Greenhayes development took place in the 1960s because it was said at the time to be the last remaining section of the hedge that, together with walls, surrounded the lands of Woking Lodge, owned by a Mr. Rastrict. He sold it off so that the new town of Woking could be developed there; it's like a 'foundation stone' to the town. Rastrict's name, spelt backwards, and the date 1868 can be found on a plaque in the remaining bit.

Also in Woking Borough is a very long hedge, over-run with Ivy, that stretches down the length of *Broadway* at Knaphill. This marks the boundary of Brookwood Hospital, one of the county's famous old mental health institutions, now redeveloped. Hopefully that hedge will be maintained for its local history interest.

Holly hedges take a long time to reach a size suited to their intended purpose yet they can be ripped out so fast. Single trees on protected land fare much better. The simple green pyramidal one at the east end of the churchyard at Lingfield catches the eye. It is well clothed in foliage right round and down to the ground. That's how Hollies like to be, because their bark is smooth and thin, making the tree susceptible to hard frosts and sunburn, both of which can kill the living layer beneath. For contrast, there's a good collection of golden variegated trees in the churchyard of Christchurch at Esher, ideal for a quiet detour from the busy High Street.

TWO INTRODUCTIONS FROM THE FLETCHER NURSERY

Probably the most significant introduction was a Lawson's Cypress, *Chamaecyparis Lawsoniana* which has blue-green foliage, tinged bronze in winter, and is fine-leaved, being a sport of the var. *filifera*. It bears the name 'Fletcheri'. As a tiddler this conifer catches the eye of those looking for a 'dwarf' for the rock garden or sink. Whoops, not a good idea! Once its roots are happy it's off to eight feet in no time! There's also a variegated form known as 'Fletcher's White' and one tinged yellow in summer known as 'Fletcheri Somerset' or just 'Somerset'.

Fletcher's nursery also introduced, in 1906, a 'dwarf' (2m) form of the Douglas Fir, *Pseudotsuga Menziesii*. It is in fact a sport from the subspecies *glauca*. It too bears the name 'Fletcheri'

Ottershaw. Chobham Rd.
green & gold Hollies.

SPRUCE

Norway Spruce - Picea abies (L) Karsten
Sitka Spruce - Picea sitchensis (Bong.) Carrière

Spruce trees are thought to get their name from Pruce or Prussia, from where the timber was imported, as it was from other northern European sources. They are not native trees; most of the species that have naturalised in Britain come from either the Far East or from the New World. Only *Picea abies* comes from Northern Europe. We have called it the *Norway* Spruce for over 200 years as that was one country of origin. In other words, it's more of a trade name than anything else. It has a number of synonyms since specific ports from which the ships departed also gave their name to the cargo. Thus it is not always clear exactly which timber is involved, let alone which specific tree. Even when the old records look specific we need to remember that names like Spruce, Pine or Fir all got used loosely.

People who despair that they cannot tell one conifer from another are highly likely to have encountered the Norway Spruce because it is used as 'Christmas Tree'. The first Christmas Trees in England arrived about the year 1800 from Germany and were Yew trees. In 1841 Prince Albert changed them to Spruce trees. He did *not* invent them, *nor* introduce them, as is so often said. The idea goes back to at least the 8th century and the legends of St. Boniface in Germany, who is credited with having cut down a sacred ancestoral Oak tree and supplanted it with a 'fir' tree. Its evergreen nature symbolised Christianity. It is believed he used a Yew tree as that is the tree that was used thereafter. The first candles on the tree are attributed to Martin Luther. Generations later people like Wordsworth and Coleridge wrote home descriptions of the German Christmas trees and then our German Queen, Charlotte of Mecklenburg-Strelitz, wife of George III, remembered the trees of her childhood and introduced the idea into England at a Christmas celebration in White Lodge, Windsor, about 1800. She made the scene so impressive news of it spread rapidly through the south, while in the north, at about the same time,

German merchants of the Hanseatic League also introduced the idea. Soon England was having Christmas Trees to rival the Holly or the Kissing Bough as the focal point of the seasonal celebrations. The idea caught on very fast. Within a few years there are references to their sale in Covent Garden Market.

Surrey adopted the new tree but many households still clung to the traditional Holly bough as their focal point, until at least the 1950s. In the post-war years the Spruce rapidly superseded it as they were much grown in the county - the last tree to be grown in the county as a crop. What was needed was a quick cash crop that was not labour intensive, bearing in mind the shortage of labour after the war and all the extra acres of land that had come into cultivation as part of the war effort. Christmas Trees provided the solution and there were both large and small plantations all over the county. Gradually they have declined and are now becoming decidedly scarce.

Other spruce trees have been tried for the same market, in the hope of finding one less inclined to drop its needles. Thus the Sitka Spruce from Alaska was tried but it doesn't flourish in S. E. England. It prefers the wetter climate of S. W. Scotland.

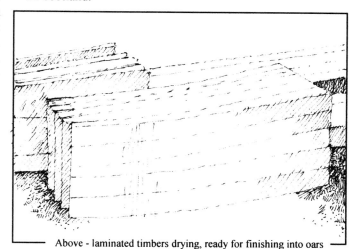

Above - laminated timbers drying, ready for finishing into oars
Below - the subtle curves of the finished oar

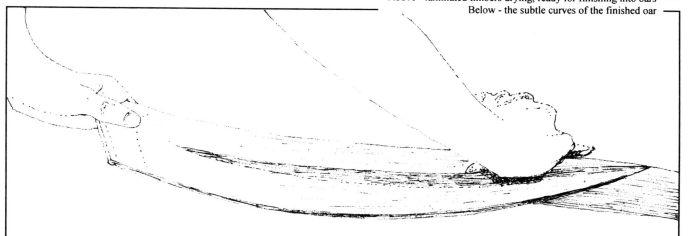

Other spruce trees have been tried for the same market, in the hope of finding one less inclined to drop its needles. Thus the Sitka Spruce from Alaska was tried but it doesn't flourish in S. E. England. It prefers the wetter climate of S. W. Scotland.

Commercially, it is an important timber tree and near Chertsey Mr Jerry Sutton has a very specialised use for it. He makes oars, not any old oars but among the very finest. These are the oars of the Oxford and Cambridge Boat Race and the Olympic Games.

It is so rare for anyone to want Sitka Spruce in very long lengths that Jerry Sutton has to import his own from Alaska or British Colombia, into Liverpool Docks or sometimes Bristol, and from there it's transported to his Thames-side yard. Home-grown timber doesn't grow fast enough to get the desired lengths knot-free, so, it's bought in as "clear and better" but even so, there's no choice in what arrives. It is therefore sorted into two qualities: the best is reserved for the *looms* or shafts of the oars and the rest is for the blade attachments, since oars are not made from one piece but are constructed. By building up the structure the poorer pieces can be incorporated within the structure without loss of quality but even so there is about 10% wastage, 20% sometimes and it's not cheap in the first place. It's dearer than hardwoods.

Jerry Sutton formerly used hardwood in the oars too. It was a fine-grained timber called Kapur, from Singapore and Malaysia but this is no longer available due to a beetle that might get imported with it. Instead, Ash is used. It is laminated into the looms to reduce compression. It's also used for tipping the blades to stop any splitting. Sadly English Ash is too irregular and not available in long lengths of high quality, so American Ash has to be imported.

Until a few years ago the timber was cut into 3in x 3in lengths and air dried ready for constructing the looms as a hollow box. Nowadays it is cut smaller at 1.5in x 3in. From this it takes five laminations to achieve the desired strength, which means taking a 350lb strain safely. Next the *cheeks* or blade sides are attached, in square section for strength. The result is crude and ugly, barely recognisable as an oar but now the craftsmen start to show their real skills. The square looms are rounded and reduced to 1.75in. diameter and roughened for a good grip. The blocks that will become the blades are marked from a template and then rounded and shaped. This is where the craftsmen really show their skills for this is high precision work. Sculls are made in pairs that must be absolutely identical, while oars are made in *sets* where each of the pair is either left or right, achieved by shaving away just two degrees of pitch off the square. When it comes to designing the hollow the craftsman shows his real worth for he must achieve a concave surface of the highest efficiency yet at the same time giving the easiest of entries and extractions from the water.

Modern conveniences, such as a band saw, are of no use for this work. The prime tool is an ancient one - the draw knife. Nothing else is so adaptable to the cutting, shaping and smoothing of the subtle curves and surfaces but above all there's no substitute for the sensitivity of the craftsmen's hands. Feeling and smoothing, they seem to massage the blade to perfection. Two coats of paint and four coats of varnish and they're ready.

view from coopers Hill.

ACKNOWLEDGEMENTS

Thanks are extended warmly to all those who, over the years, have shared their knowledge, skills and interests to open my eyes wider. In particular I extend grateful thanks to Michael Dennett, Jerry Sutton and Bob Underdown, and their fellow workers, for allowing me to feature them and their craftsmanship in the book. For specialist help in checking the final text I would like to thank, in alphabetical order: Julian Abraham, Arboriculture Officer, Woking Borough Council; Penny Hollow for Haslemere Educational Museum; Martin Humphrey, Surrey Chairman, International Tree Foundation; Jenny King, Surrey Gardens Trust; Sally Kington, RHS Library; Brenda Lewis, Historic Parks and Gardens Officer, Surrey County Council; Robert McGibbon, Surrey Heathland Project; Doug. Richards, Horticultural Manager, Woking Borough Council.

For studio assistance in producing the final manuscript: Sue Harvey; Hazel Putland; James Findlay; Gordon Weaver.

SOURCES

Most of the basic material in this book has been collected on site and through conversations, over many years, with people more knowlegeable than myself. Often it started with a slight reference in a book or just an entry on an inventory, for which a full bibliography would be of little help to readers seeking more information. Until 1998 the best advice has always been to start at the Surrey Local Studies Library at Guildford but that has now moved to Woking as part of the new Surrey History Centre, which has with it the Surrey Record Office and material from the former Guildford Muniment Room. Here you will find the histories of the places of Surrey and the materials and facilities for more extensive research. Below are listed a selection of books used plus others that introduce readers to the uses of trees.

BOOK LIST

Brimble, L. J. F., *Trees in Britain*, MacMillan, 1948
Chetan, A. and D. Brueton, *The Sacred Yew*, Arkana, 1994
Cox, J. C., *Churchwardens' Accounts*, Methuen, 1913
Edlin, Herbert, *Woodland Crafts in Britain*, Country Book Club, 1974
Evelyn, John, *Silva or a Discourse of Forest-trees*, 1662
Galinou, M. ed., *London's Pride - The Glorious History of the Capital's Gardens*, Anaya Publishers Ltd, 1990.
Grigson, Geoffrey, *A Dictionary of English Plant Names*, Allen Lane, 1973
Humphrey, Martin, *Woking: Tree Heritage Rambles*, Chris Howkins; 1990
Johnson, C. P., *The Useful Plants of Great Britain*, Hardwicke, 1862.
Leslie, A.C. *Flora of Surrey: Supplement and Checklist*, A.C.& P.Leslie, Guildford, 1987.
Lewington, Anna, *Plants for People*, Natural History Museum, 1990
Loudon, J. C., *In Search of English Gardens: The Travels of John Claudius Loudon and his Wife Jane*, ed. Priscilla Boniface, Lennard Publishing, 1987
Maclean, T. *Medieval English Gardens*, Collins, 1981
Mabey, Richard, *Flora Britannica*, Sinclair-Stevenson, 1996
Mitchell, Alan; *A Field Guide to the Trees of Britain and Northern Europe*; Collins, 2nd ed. 1978
Roach, F. A., *Cultivated Fruits of Britain: Their Origin and History*, Blackwell, 1985
Royal Horticultural Society, *Dictionary of Gardening*, 1992
Rackham, Oliver, *History of the Countryside*, Dent, 1986
Veitch, James; *A Manual of Coniferae*, London, 1881
Vickery, Roy, *A Dictionary of Plant Lore*, OUP, 1995
Wilks, J. H., *Trees of the British Isles in History and Legend*, Muller, 1972.
Young, Geoffrey, *Traditional British Crafts*, Marshall Cavendish, 1989

INDEX

Trees by English names, Places in Surrey, Selected subjects.

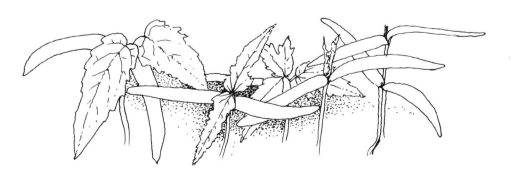

May
Hawthorn